D0932627

Printed in the United States of America

Table of Contents

Introduction

The National Association of Legal Assistants was established in 1970. The CP Certified Paralegal and CLA Certified Legal Assistant Examinations were established by the National Association of Legal Assistants (NALA) in 1976. According to the NALA website, as of November 2013, there are over 17,711 Certified Paralegals and over 3,000 Advanced Certified Paralegals in the United States.

Although there were thousands of paralegal and legal assistant programs in the United States until the exam was established, there was no standardized measurement of what a paralegal learned or needed to know in order to be considered certified in his or her field. Paralegals and legal assistants have qualifications that range from high school education with no formal training to years of legal secretarial work experience to AA, BS and MA degrees in Legal Studies to persons with Juris Doctorate degrees that preferred to work as paralegals rather than practice law. In essence, there was no uniformity and no standards in the field.

The CLA exam provides the means for establishing uniformity and minimum standards within the field. Even though the exams are nationwide, some state bars still administer their own paralegal/legal assistant exam. The exam is given three times per year in January, May and September.

The exam was originally set up to test applicants in five areas: Communication, Ethics, Judgment and Analytical Ability, Legal Research and Substantive Law. The original substantive law section consisted of American Legal system plus four other specialty areas. Applicants had the chance to select four out of nine specialty areas.

In September 2013, the exam changed to restrict the substantive areas to the following: American Legal System, Business Organizations, Civil Litigation and Contracts.

According to the NALA results issued November 2013, the percentage of points required to pass are as follows: Communications: 79%, Ethics: 81%, Judgment and Analytical Ability: 77%, Legal Research: 76% and Substantive Law: 78%. The total points for each part are as follows: Communications: 75, Ethics: 75, Judgment and Analytical Ability: 150, Legal Research: 50 and Substantive Law: 200.

This manual is intended to give students an overview of the material that will be tested on the exam, as well as provide practice questions for the individual sections, including an enhanced focus on communication issues, because this is where students tend to lose the most ground. Most students focus on the substantive law areas of the test, but if a paralegal is not well versed in grammar rules, vocabulary and formal writing, he or she will do herself and her employer a great disservice.

Good luck!

I. COMMUNICATIONS

Jargon, Slang and Colloquialisms

Jargon

Jargon is defined as the language used for a particular activity or by a particular group of people. It is very common in legal writing – indeed, there is a term that refers to legal jargon as "legalese". Most people in the United States hear some form of legal jargon every day. Newspapers, media and popular entertainment, such as fictional shows about police or law, use legal jargon to enhance their own credibility. The problem with jargon is that a large portion of the population may be familiar with the term, but may not fully understand it. Therefore, jargon or "legalese" should always be fully explained in legal writing.

Some examples of legal jargon are "the case is on all fours" which means the case has significantly similar facts/issues, rationales, arguments and holdings that can be used to support a case.

Slang

Slang is defined by the Merriam Webster Dictionary as "words that are not considered part of the standard vocabulary of a language and that are used very informally in speech, especially by a particular group of people." It does not have a place in formal legal writing, but in recent years, it has crept in. Slang is most commonly found today in deposition transcripts and trial transcripts, because these two types of documents reflect the actual words of the witnesses. Since the attorneys cannot ask the witness to utilize non-colloquial English when giving testimony, the transcripts contain some slang. Most attorneys and indeed some judges will ask the witness to explain or clarify the definition of a slang term so that the witness' meaning is clearly understood.

Colloquialisms

Colloquialisms are defined by Merriam Webster as: "a local or regional dialect expression." Essentially, this is region-specific slang. For instance, farmers may say "living high off the hog" to describe someone who is rich and leads a comfortable life, because they are familiar with pigs – though someone who grew up in a big city may not understand the expression. Colloquialisms are best avoided in legal writing because they are location-specific. A colloquial expression in Kansas may mean something different in Maine. Other examples of colloquialisms include "Subway Series" in New York (meaning a game played between the Mets and the Yankees,) or a Southerner expressing his or her excitement by exclaiming "Great day in the morning!"

Slang, jargon and colloquialisms are commonly used in everyday language, but a paralegal should try to minimize their use his or her legal writing.

Grammar and Parts of Speech

This section is a quick review of the parts of speech you learned in high school, but here, we will focus on those parts of speech that create the majority of problems for legal writers.
The basics are easy to remember and learn. Let's get started:

- *Nouns.* Nouns name a person, place, thing or idea/concept. Proper nouns include names of persons and places. These are easily recognizable because they are usually capitalized. Examples of proper nouns are: Jared, Karen, Paris, Ohio and Zen Buddhism. Examples of regular common nouns are: boy, dog, gorilla, buffet, courthouse, university and sigma.

- *Verbs.* Verbs show action or a state of being. There are helping, auxiliary and linking verbs that link the subject to another word. Some examples of action verbs: run, argued, ate, won, hypothesized and extrapolated. Examples of linking verbs include am, is, being, was and were. There are other "action" verbs that can function as linking verbs as well. They include: look, taste, feel, appear, sound, seems, smell, grow, remain and stay.

    - *Auxiliary Verbs.* Also known as "helping" verbs, these help other verbs (usually of the action variety.) This combination of auxiliary verbs and main verbs create verb phrases. The auxiliary/helping verb lists include the following: be, can, do, have, may, might, must, shall, should, will and would.

    - *Verb conjugation.* The form of a verb is changed by tense, number, mood and voice. An example of verbs affected by tense: I am running – present tense, I ran yesterday- past tense and I will run tomorrow –future tense. An example of verbs affected by number : She thinks that she is very intelligent –singular, present tense form of the verb "think." They think that the test was too long - plural present tense form of the verb "think."

    - *Verb moods.* There are four verb moods: the infinitive, the subjunctive, the imperative and the indicative mood. The infinitive mood is just the basic verb form without regard to tense, number, or any other conjugations to link this form to the subject. This form is often referred to as the "to" form of the verb because it almost always appears with the word to preceding the verb. The subjunctive mood of a verb can provide a reader with the explanation or necessity of an action. The subjunctive mood is a great tool used in legal writing, especially in opening and closing statements. The imperative mood is used to convey a command and the word "you" is most often implied instead of written. The indicative mood is not a command and the verb contains explanatory or emphatic modifiers.

- *Voice.* The last conjugation that troubles most legal writers is the concept of voice. There are two voices in the English language - the active voice and the passive voice. The active voice conveys an action that a subject performs. For example: The student is taking notes in class. The passive voice fails to identify the subject taking the action. The passive voice of this statement is: Notes are taken in class. Problems usually arise when legal writers use the passive voice in the past tense, because there are many similarities in past-tense conjugations. However, it is a simple concept once you grasp that in any sentence, *someone or something* must perform the action. If you describe the action but not the actor, you are likely writing in passive voice.

- *Past Participle*. The past participle is usually the "ed" form of regular verbs that can be used as adjectives or modifiers. An example of past participles that can be used as adjectives include, for instance, the word *exhausted*. "Exhaust" is a verb in this case, but in the past tense it becomes a past participle and can be used as an adjective to describe a person's state.

There are other rules that involve forms of verbs: verbals, gerunds, and more – and we will discuss these a little later.

- *Pronouns.* A pronoun takes the place of a noun. The main thing to remember about pronouns is that they must always refer or relate back to a specific preceding word (called the antecedent.)
    - Personal pronouns include I, me, you we, he, she, it, us, and they
    - Possessive pronouns include my, mine, our(s), your(s), her(s), his, their(s) and its
    - Interrogative pronouns include who, whom, whose, which, and what
    - Relative pronouns include who, whom, whose, which, and that
    - Demonstrative pronouns include that, this, those, and these

- Reflexive or intensive pronouns include myself, yourself, himself, herself, itself, ourselves, yourselves, and themselves

- Indefinite pronouns include some, all, many, each, one, none, everyone, everything, everybody, anyone, anything, anybody, somebody, someone, something, no one, nothing, and nobody.

- *Prepositions*. A preposition is word that shows the relationship between a noun or pronoun and some other word in the sentence or phrase. Some of the most common prepositions are at, above, beyond, after, over, in, under, beside, off, of, and with. Prepositions combine with other words to make prepositional phrases. The phrases always start with the preposition and end with the object of the preposition. For example: "Under the boardwalk" is a prepositional phrase.

- *Adjectives.* An adjective modifies a noun. Adjectives are descriptive words that answer descriptive questions, such as what kind, how many, and which one. Examples of adjectives include slow, devastating, cold and tasty.

- *Adverbs.* An adverb is a word that modifies a verb, an adjective or another adverb. Adverbs tell how and in what manner. They alter or change the meaning of verbs, adjectives and any other part of speech that addresses. Adverbs often end in "ly". Some examples of adverbs are: never, slowly, after, seldom, often and now.

- *Conjunctions*. Conjunctions are little words with big functions. They are responsible for holding much larger parts of speech together. There are three types of conjunctions:

  - *Coordinating*. These conjunctions are for, and, nor, but, or, yet and so. They are easy to remember if you use the acronym FANBOYS.

  - *Subordinating*. The subordinating conjunction joins a dependent clause to an independent clause. Examples of subordinating conjunctions are: after, lest, because, in case and once.

  - *Correlative*. These conjunctions perform the same function as the coordinating conjunctions, but they are always used in pairs. Examples of correlative conjunctions include not only, but also, either or, neither nor, and whether or.

- *Gerunds.* A verbal is a form of verb that functions as another part of speech. We have touched a little on infinitives and participles, but one of the most difficult verbals is known as the gerund. A gerund is the (ing) form of a verb that functions as a noun. For example: "Reading is my greatest joy." Normally, the word reading would be consider an active tense of the verb "to read." Here, reading is used in the same way that one would utilize a noun. In other words, reading becomes a verb dressed up like a noun while remaining a verb. A gerund is akin to a hybrid of the two other parts of speech. It should be noted that whereas all gerunds end in (ing), it is sometimes difficult to distinguish gerunds from participles that also end in (ing). The major difference between a gerund and a participle is that a gerund functions as a noun, but a participle is a verb form that functions as an adjective.

Capitalization Rules

- The first word of a sentence is capitalized regardless of its status or part of speech.

- The first letter of proper nouns is always capitalized

- The first letter of words that modify proper nouns must be capitalized. For instance, when we refer to someone's uncle, the word is not capitalized. When we refer to a specific uncle, i.e., Uncle Murray, we must capitalize "uncle."

- The first letter of each word in the title of a document, book, film, etc. must be capitalized. Rules vary within different academic styles, but in legal writing, each word must be capitalized with the exception of "a," "an," all prepositions and all coordinating conjunctions.

- Months are capitalized, but not the names of the seasons.

- Some names include words that are not capitalized, including Edward von Morrison and Oscar de la Hoya. It may be helpful for you to know that these words usually mean "of" or "of the," neither of which we would capitalize in the title of a book. If you think of a name as the "title" of a person, you won't forget this rule.

Commonly Confused/Misused Words

Another section that causes problems for CPA/CLA test takers is the section on confused and misused words. This section is very important because one word that is misused can and does change the entire meaning of a law, letter or any other type of legal document.

The list of confused words includes:

- Accept: This word is a verb that means to receive
- Except: This word is a preposition that means to leave out or exclude

- Advice: A noun that means a suggestion or opinion about what to do
- Advise: A verb that means to give ideas, suggestions or advice.

- Affect: A verb that means to bring about a change or to exert influence over a matter. In rare cases, it is used as a noun (often by psychologists) to describe a person's demeanor.
- Effect: A noun that describes the results of an action. In rare cases, it is used as a verb in the same way as "affect," but not in legal writing.

- All ready: A descriptive phrase that refers to everyone or everything having completed all preparations.
- Already: Refers to an act that occurred prior to a specific time

- Among: A preposition that refers to three or more persons, ideas, events, etc
- Between: A preposition used when referring to two persons, ideas, events, etc

- Bare: An adjective that means without covering or protection
- Bear: A big, furry, animal.

- Amount: Term used to refer to things that are not usually or easily separated: i.e. oil, water, wine
- Number: Term used to refer to items that can enumerated individually: i.e. humans, dogs, mangoes

- Anxious: Adjective that means worried or ill at ease
- Eager: Adjective that means having a great desire or keen expectancy towards an upcoming event

- Ball: A noun referring to a round or sphere-shaped object used in games
- Bawl: A verb that means to cry, sob or weep loudly

- Boll: A noun that refers to the pod or seed of a plant i.e., a cotton boll
- Bowl: A noun that refers to a round dish that holds food

- Brake: A noun that refers to a mechanism used to slow down a vehicle. Can also be a verb that refers to the act of slowing down a vehicle
- Break : A noun that means a pause or interruption in an activity or event. Can also be a verb that means to separate into smaller pieces or to interrupt

- Chili: A noun that that refers to small peppers or to a dish made of peppers, meat and usually beans
- Chilly: An adjective that describes a temperature that is cooler than warm but not freezing or cold

- Choose: The present tense of the verb that means to pick or select.
- Chose: The past tense of the verb "choose"

- Complement: This term can be a noun or a verb that means to complete or bring to fruition.
- Compliment: This term also can be a noun or a verb that means to give accolades or praise(verb) or it can refer to the actual words of praise(noun)

- Conscience: A noun that refers to the awareness of right and wrong, good and evil, just and unjust
- Conscious: An adjective that means to be awake or aware of one's surroundings

- Come : A verb that means to approach or draw closer
- Cum: A Latin preposition used between to objects to indicate joinder or something of a combined nature

- Dear : This word can be a noun, adjective or adverb that usually signifies affection, a salutation at the beginning of a letter, or reference to an expensive item or event
- Deer: A quadruped animal

- Disinterested: An adjective that means objective or impartial
- Uninterested: An adjective that coveys a lack of desire to know about a person or subject

- Fewer: An adjective used to refer to items that are counted separately i.e. : fewer tests, nurses, melons
- Less : An adjective or adverb that refers to items that cannot be counted separately: air, noise, pollution. Less also works as an adverb.

- Hear: A verb that means registering or perceiving sound by ear
- Here: An adverb that refers to a place, point or position.

- Lead: This word can be a noun: a chemical element, or an example for others to follow. I can also be a verb that means to be in charge of, or exert authority, over others
- Led: Past tense of the verb "lead"

- Loose: This term can be an adjective which means not fitting tightly, or it can be a verb that means to free or to liberate
- Lose: A verb that refers to the inability to find an object or a person

- Passed: This is the past tense of the verb to pass which means to move in a particular direction
- Past: This is a noun that refers to a prior time period

- Personal: An adjective that means individual or private
- Personnel: A noun that refers to persons or staff that are part of an organization

- Precede: A verb that means to happen or go before
- Proceed: A verb that means to continue or to advance

- Principal: A noun that could refer to the person in charge of a school, or an adjective that means most important or first
- Principle: A noun that refers to a law, doctrine or strong belief

- Quit: A verb that means to cease or refrain from doing a particular action
- Quite : An adverb that indicates a very high degree , completely or totally
- Quiet: An adjective that refers to the absence of noise or silence

- Some: Can be a pronoun that refers to indeterminate amount or number, or it can be an adverb that refers to extent
- Sum: A noun that refers to the result of adding two numbers or items

- Than : A conjunction used to make comparisons
- Then : An adverb that can mean next, or shortly thereafter

- Their : A possessive pronoun that indicates ownership
- There: An adverb that refers to a place that is not where one is currently located
- They're: A contraction for the words "they are"

- Threw: Past tense of the verb "throw"
- Through: A preposition that means to travel from one side to the other
- Thru: A shortened misspelling of the word "through"

- To: A preposition indicating direction
- Too: An adverb that means in addition to, also or a lot
- Two: An adjective that refers to more than one item but less than three. It can also be a noun that refers to more than one person

- We're : A contraction of the words we are
- Were : A past tense of a helping verb

- Where: An adverb that indicates place or position
- Wear: A verb that means to put on one's body, as in apparel, or to erode or damage

- Your: A possessive pronoun that indicates ownership
- You're: A contraction for the words you are

Punctuation

The CP/CLA test will examine how well you understand when and how to use various punctuation symbols.

The Apostrophe

An apostrophe is used to form contractions and to show possession for all singular and indefinite pronouns. The first use is illustrated in the following manner: "You're really becoming an expert in legal research."

The word "you're" is a contraction for the words you are. The use of the apostrophe lets the reader know that the implied meaning is you are but that the "a" has been omitted.

Some common contractions include: Aren't , Can't, Couldn't, Didn't, Doesn't, Don't, Hasn't, Haven't, I'm, Isn't ,It's, Let's, They're, Wasn't, Weren't, Won't, and You're.

The second use of an apostrophe is to show possession as is illustrated in the following manner: The attorney's office was a mess. The use of the apostrophe in this sentence indicates that the attorney owns the office. The apostrophe is also used to show possession for indefinite pronouns: "Everyone's eyes stung from the smoke."

There are three very important rules to remember when using apostrophes:

1. Do not use an apostrophe when writing a personal possessive pronoun. A common mistake is to write the word "yours" as your's.

2. Sentences that refer to amounts of money or time usually require an apostrophe . For instance: "I really do not want to hear your two cents' worth of advice." "It is all in a day's work."

3. Plural possessive nouns that end in "s" need an apostrophe at the end. "The Harris' trial lasted one month." However, an apostrophe and an "s" should be added to plural nouns that do not end in "s": example: The group's noise was excessive.

The Bracket

The bracket is generally used to help clarify the meaning of words, and is often used interchangeably with the parenthesis (depending on the academic style.) This clarification can be in the form of indicating a misspelling or typo i.e. [judgement] or it can be used to add emphasis or make an editorial comment i.e. "Her large [Antebellum] house looked like Tara's from *Gone With the Wind.*" The bracket, used in pairs, can be used to add a prefix, suffix or explanatory word in order to adapt a quote to your sentence i.e.: "Music is [our] only love." Brackets can also be used to change the tense of a verb in a quote to make a writer's sentences parallel and balanced, i.e. eat[ing], drink[ing] and be[ing] merry are actions guaranteed to make one happy.

The Colon and Semicolon

The colon (:) and the semicolon (;) are two punctuation marks that are commonly confused in formal writing. Colons are used to indicate lists, series and examples. Colons are also used to link two main clauses if the second clause is an explanation or example of the first clause, i.e. "The office was a nightmare for the paralegal: law books were all over the floor, case files were strewn across the desk, and the chair was stacked with unopened mail."

The semicolon should be used to link two independent clauses provided that they are not joined by a coordinating conjunction, i.e. "Two hundred students applied for law school; only fifty of the students were accepted." Both of these phrases could stand alone as sentences, but for stylistic reasons, the author may choose to put them in the same sentence, perhaps in order to make the reader infer a connection between the phrases where it is not immediately apparent. Semicolons are not used to separate subordinate clauses – in those cases, a comma is appropriate.

Other Punctuation Marks

- The period (.) is the punctuation mark used to denote the end of a sentence with no special cases.

- The question mark (?) is used at the end of an interrogative sentence or one that asks a direct question. It is not used in sentences that ask indirect questions. For example: "Did you read the brief?" is correct. "I am perplexed as to why he included her name on the witness list?" is not correct, because this sentence refers to an indirect question.

- The exclamation mark or point (!) is used after short sentences, phrases and even after single words to show strong feelings or emotions. For example: "Hallelujah!" "Oh my God, a snake!"

- The hyphen (-) is a punctuation mark that is used in compound words that have a combined meaning, and to divide or break a word at the end of a line. If a hyphen is used to divide a word, it should be divided at a break in the syllables. An example of a hyphen used in a compound word is "part-time." Hyphens are commonly used now in many proper names: Sharon Thomas-Webb, Esq. The rules for hyphens will change in the future when children born with hyphenated names start to marry other children with hyphenated names.

- Parenthesis () is a punctuation mark closely related to the bracket. They are used in pairs to include information that would not normally appear in the sentence. One rule to remember about parenthesis involves ending punctuation marks: If the text within the parenthesis is a complete sentence, then the ending punctuation mark goes inside the parenthesis. For example: I like to read opinions written by 19th century justices (John Marshall is my favorite Supreme Court Justice.) If the text within the parenthesis is not a complete sentence then the punctuation mark goes after the parentheses i.e.: I use Lexis (not Westlaw).

- Rules regarding quotation marks (") are a little more complicated than some of the other punctuation marks. Quotation marks are used to set aside or enclose direct quotations; they are not used in indirect quotations. For example, Patrick Henry said "Give me liberty or give me death." Another rule to remember is that periods and commas are placed inside quotation marks (Please see the above example.) However, colons and semi colons are placed outside of the quotation marks. Another important rule to remember is that a question mark goes inside quotation marks if the text is a question, but the quotation marks are outside the question mark if the quotation is not a question, even if the whole sentence is. Examples: The spoiled child asked, "Where is my candy?" The second part of the rule is exemplified by: Did the judge say "I am holding both parties in contempt."? Finally, if a quote within a quote is needed then the outside quotation is enclosed by double quotation marks and the inside quotation is enclosed by single quotation marks. For example: The professor asked "How does the Miranda Court interpret 'custodial interrogation' in relation to arrests?"

- The ellipsis (...) is a punctuation mark that is seen fairly often in legal writing, but the name is not familiar to a lot of the users of this mark. An ellipsis is comprised of three dots evenly spaced apart, used to let the reader know that part of a quotation has been left out or omitted. It used in legal writing when a direct quote needs to be used, but the writer only wants to reference part of the quote, not the entire section. The use of the ellipsis serves to maintain brevity and conciseness in legal writing. For example: The concept of separate but equal... was abolished in 1954.

- The most difficult punctuation mark is the comma (,) which accounts more punctuation errors than all other punctuation marks combined. The comma is used to join main clauses, parts of sentences, words in series, adjectives, adverbs, nouns, verbs and just about any part of speech. Commas are also used after introductory words and transitional expressions. Some common introductory words are: yes, no, indeed, next, first, however, additionally, therefore, nevertheless and similarly. Common transitional words include: in fact, for example, as a result, in other words, and on the other hand. Commas are used after all participial phrases and introductory infinitive phrases. Example: Deafened by the noise, the puppy hid beneath the bed. Entire books have been written about comma usage; therefore it is evident this punctuation mark requires your studious attention. When in doubt, always refer to the dictionary. No discussion of commas would be complete without proper homage to the bane of most writers' existence: the comma splice. A comma splice occurs when a punctuation mark is used to link together or splice two independent phrases that could stand on their own as complete sentences. An example of comma splice: Terry studied a long time for her exam, Carl partied all night before the test, and Travis forgot to show up for the test. The comma splice is between the text regarding Terry's actions and Carl's actions. "Terry studied a long time for her exam" and "Carl partied all night before the test" are both independent phrases that can stand on their own as complete sentences.

There is a lot of information available online that explains in-depth the use of punctuation marks; this section is provided as a quick review of some of the common problems encountered with punctuation usage in legal writing.

Vocabulary

The vocabulary section on most standardized tests presents a challenge to test takers because the exam is usually packed with archaic, multisyllabic words that nobody uses anymore. To make matters worse, the legal vocabulary aptitude tests are crammed with Latin words that most courts don't even use anymore. This is of no concern to the test creators, so most students settle in to "learn" the definition of hundreds of words in a few weeks. There is a better way to study for the vocabulary test.

The best way to quickly discern the meanings of unfamiliar words is to dissect or take apart the word. That may sound daunting but once you learn the process, it is simple.

The first thing that you have to remember is that most multisyllabic words have three parts:

- *Prefix.* Dictionary.com defines prefix as: An affix that is placed before the word and that, although not a word itself, can be bound to the base of a word, to form a derivative with a related meaning. Entire families of related words can derive from an existing word in this way. A list of common prefixes is easy to learn and once you know their meaning, you are on the right road to discerning the meaning of the word.

- *Suffix.* The next part that you need to know is the suffix. A suffix is similar to a prefix except that it is added to the end of the word not the beginning of the root word.

- *Root.* The hardest part of the word to figure out will be the root word or the main part of the word. These words are often referred to as cognates, which means that they come from a similar family or origin. This is very helpful information when a student needs to learn the meaning of a word.

Now that the process is simplified, it will be much easier to learn a list of common prefixes, suffixes and cognates than to try to memorize hundreds of vocabulary words. There is a list of prefixes and suffixes at the Englishclub website (www.englishclub.com.) Other websites can provide you with lists and meanings; this website has a good format and is designed for students and teachers of English.

There is an excellent list of root words listed at www.learnthat.org. This website boasts that it is the largest root word and prefix directory. It is very extensive and will provide you with most of the root words that you will ever need to learn.

Regular vocabulary terms aren't terribly difficult, but legal vocabulary can be quite frustrating. Most legal terms come from Latin, which is called a "dead language." This means you will have to learn Latin cognates.

Don't despair! There are good websites that list most legal terms and their meanings. The website www.inrebus.com provides students with a plethora of Latin legal words and maxims. Not only is this site a good resource to study, it is a great reference tool to have at one's disposal after you have completed the transition from student to professional.

List of Words and Definitions

Below is a list of GRE vocabulary words from **http://www.testprepreview.com/vocabulary.htm** that will allow you to practice your skills discerning the meaning of certain words based upon prefixes, suffixes and root words. Since these words are regularly used on graduate exams, it may be in your best interest to commit some of the words and definitions to memory. The ones that do not adhere to the root word, prefix, and suffix dissection process would be great choices for memorization.

- **adumbrate:** To represent beforehand in outline or by emblem.
- **alacrity:** Cheerful willingness.
- **animadversion:** The utterance of criticism or censure.
- **antediluvian:** Of or pertaining to the times, things, events before the great flood in the days of Noah.
- **apotheosis:** Deification.
- **bumptious:** Full of offensive and aggressive self-conceit.
- **calumny:** Slander.
- **coeval:** Existing during the same period of time; also, a contemporary
- **Cogitate:** Consider carefully and deeply; ponder.
- **comestible:** Fit to be eaten.
- **complaisance:** Politeness.
- **denouement:** That part of a play or story in which the mystery is cleared up.
- **desuetude:** A state of disuse or inactivity.
- **edacious:** Given to eating.
- **effulgence:** Splendor.
- **encomium:** A formal or discriminating expression of praise.
- **euphonious:** Characterized by agreeableness of sound.
- **fugacious:** Fleeting.
- **fulminate:** To cause to explode.
- **grandiloquent:** Speaking in or characterized by a pompous or bombastic style.
- **gregarious:** Sociable, outgoing
- **iconoclast:** An image-breaker.
- **imbroglio:** A misunderstanding attended by ill feeling, perplexity, or strife.
- **imbue :** To dye; to instill profoundly.
- **impecunious:** Having no money.

- **inchoate:** Incipient.
- **incipient:** Initial.
- **inimical:** Adverse.
- **junta:** A council or assembly that deliberates in secret upon the affairs of government.
- **lachrymose:** Given to shedding tears.
- **loquacious:** Talkative.
- **lugubrious:** Indicating sorrow, often ridiculously.
- **mellifluous:** Sweetly or smoothly flowing.
- **mendacious:** Untrue.
- **mendicant:** A beggar.
- **meretricious:** Alluring by false or gaudy show.
- **munificent:** Extraordinarily generous.
- **myriad:** A vast indefinite number.
- **nadir:** The lowest point.
- **nefarious:** Wicked in the extreme.
- **nugatory:** Having no power or force.
- **obdurate:** Impassive to feelings of humanity or pity.
- **obfuscate:** To darken; to obscure.
- **obsequious:** Showing a servile readiness to fall in with the wishes or will of another.
- **obstreperous:** Boisterous.
- **obtrude:** To be pushed or to push oneself into undue prominence.
- **opprobrium:** The state of being scornfully reproached or accused of evil.
- **ossify:** To convert into bone.
- **ostentation:** A display dictated by vanity and intended to invite applause or flattery.
- **ostracism:** Exclusion from intercourse or favor, as in society or politics.
- **panegyric:** A formal and elaborate eulogy, written or spoken, of a person or of an act.
- **panoply:** A full set of armor.
- **pellucid:** Translucent.
- **penury:** Indigence.
- **peregrination:** A wandering.
- **peremptory:** Precluding question or appeal.
- **peripatetic:** Walking about.
- **pernicious:** Tending to kill or hurt.
- **persiflage:** Banter.
- **perspicacity:** Acuteness or discernment.
- **perturbation:** Mental excitement or confusion.
- **physiognomy:** The external appearance merely.
- **profligacy:** Shameless viciousness.
- **prolix:** Verbose.
- **propinquity:** Nearness.

- **propitious:** Kindly disposed.
- **prosaic:** Unimaginative.
- **puerile:** Childish.
- **quiescent:** Being in a state of repose or inaction.
- **Quixotic:** Chivalrous or romantic to a ridiculous or extravagant degree.
- **quotidian:** Of an everyday character; ordinary.
- **raconteur:** A person skilled in telling stories.
- **recondite:** Incomprehensible to one of ordinary understanding.
- **recrudescent:** Becoming raw or sore again.
- **repine:** To indulge in fretfulness and faultfinding.
- **reprobate:** One abandoned to depravity and sin.
- **salubrious:** Healthful; promoting health.
- **sanguine:** Cheerfully confident; optimistic.
- **sardonic:** Scornfully or bitterly sarcastic.
- **sedulous:** Persevering in effort or endeavor.
- **somniferous:** Tending to produce sleep.
- **somnolent:** Sleepy.
- **sonorous:** Resonant.
- **sophistry:** Reasoning sound in appearance only, especially when designedly deceptive.
- **sybarite:** A luxurious person.
- **sycophant:** A servile flatterer, especially of those in authority or influence.
- **timorous:** Lacking courage.
- **torpid:** Dull; sluggish; inactive.
- **torrid:** Excessively hot.
- **tortuous:** Abounding in irregular bends or turns.
- **truculent:** Having the character or the spirit of a savage.
- **turbid:** In a state of turmoil; muddled
- **turgid:** Swollen.
- **turpitude:** Depravity.
- **tutelage:** The act of training or the state of being under instruction.
- **tyro:** One slightly skilled in or acquainted with any trade or profession.
- **vapid:** Having lost sparkling quality and flavor.
- **variegated:** Having marks or patches of different colors; also, varied.
- **virago:** Loud talkative women, strong statured women
- **virtu:** Rare, curious, or beautiful quality.
- **vitiate:** To contaminate.
- **vituperate:** To overwhelm with wordy abuse.
- **vivify:** To endue with life.
- **vociferous:** Making a loud outcry.
- **Zeitgeist:** The intellectual and moral tendencies that characterize any age or epoch.

Human Resources and Interviewing

One task that usually falls to paralegals and legal assistants is interviewing. Paralegals perform intake interviews, witness interviews and applicant interviews. The most important trait for any interviewer is being a good listener. Being a good listener does not just involve hearing what is being said, but the ability to comprehend and apply what you have heard.

Intake Interviewer

As an intake interviewer, the paralegal is more than likely the first person to converse with a potential client other than the secretary or receptionist. In order to be an effective intake interviewer, the paralegal must be prepared for the interview. During an intake interview, notes and photographs may be taken, and disclosure agreements may be signed.

Items to keep on hand during an intake interview include pen, pencil, paper, cameras, recorders, case files and any legal documents that may need to be signed. Most importantly, you need to maintain a pleasant countenance. A smile goes a long way toward ensuring a productive interview. Patience is also a very useful tool to employ during an interview.

Since the intake interview is probably the potential client's first interaction with the firm and first impressions are lasting impressions. If an initial intake form has not been by the receptionist then the paralegal will have to elicit background and demographic information. Making sure that the client is comfortable and at ease is the key to getting an interview started off on the right foot.

Face to Face Interview Steps

Some general face to face interview steps to follow include:

1. Do not keep the client waiting if at all possible.

2. Greet the client pleasantly and offer a handshake. If you know or have reason to suspect that the client is Muslim or any other faith that prohibits physical contact between persons of the opposite sex, then please do not attempt to shake hands or make contact. If you are not sure, then it might be better to ask then to risk a handshake that would be considered offensive and insulting.

3. After the initial greeting, offer the client a seat and refreshment, if available. Small talk and pleasantries can be exchanged for about 3 to 5 minutes before that actual interview begins. If the paralegal maintains a smiling and pleasant demeanor during this chit chat session, you have a better chance of establishing positive rapport will be established smoothly transitioning into the interview.

4. It is better to have a list of interview questions written down so that important information is not overlooked or omitted. It is a good practice to memorize the first three or four

questions so that the interviewee does not feel like he or she is in an interrogation room at the local police station.

5. Before the actual questioning begins, the paralegal should explain the purpose of the questions and reassure the client that what he or she says will be held in the strictest confidence.

6. As the client speaks, listen carefully and take notes so that the client does not have to repeat their answers. If there is any ambiguity in the answers or you need, do not hesitate to ask the client to expound upon the point that needs explanation. Another good tool to use if there is a concern about a client's answers is the paraphrase. Paraphrasing the client's answers seems to work better than asking for repetition because the paraphrase ensures the client that the paralegal was listening.

7. Once the interview is completed and all needed documents are signed, the paralegal should thank the client for his or her time, provide the client with a business card or other source that can be used to follow up with the paralegal and escort him or her out of the room in which the intake interview was conducted.

Witness Interviews

The witness interview is very similar to the intake interview. However, the purpose of the witness interview is to prepare the client for giving testimony at trial or in a deposition. The paralegal must explain the purpose and nature of the questions. If the questions that will be asked are of a personal nature, the paralegal should stress that the communication is confidential.

One concept that must be stressed to clients is that there may be questions asked that will make them uncomfortable, but unless their attorney or the judge instructs them not to answer, they are required to answer. The clients should also be made aware that they are to answer truthfully only what they remember; they should be instructed not to guess or speculate regarding a question.

Clients, like most people, want to know what is going to happen so that they can prepare ahead of time. It is the paralegal's job to inform the clients that even though they are being prepared for the testimony they will give to the questions posed by their attorney, no one can prepare them for all of the questions that opposing counsel may pose. The paralegal should have researched the opposing counsel's examination style and trial practice before the witness interview so that he or she can provide the client with an accurate set of questions that the opposing counsel may ask.

When the witness interview is over, the paralegal should reassure the witness that he or she has done a fine job and will do an even better job when questioned under oath. A word of caution here: legal work is time consuming and schedules are packed. However, it is imperative that the paralegal allow the client the time or she needs to become comfortable answering the questions. Too little time spent in witness preparation interviews can be disastrous. It is far better to spend the time than to lose the case.

Paralegals generally do not have to interview hostile witnesses so instructions on dealing with hostile witnesses are not included here.

Employment Applicant Interview

Another type of interview that paralegals conduct is employee applicant interviews. These types of interviews are usually conducted by a paralegal supervisor, case manager or senior paralegal. The purpose of this type of interview is the selection of qualified applicants for employment vacancies within the firm or company.

The paralegal must read the resumes, cover letters, transcripts and reference letters of the persons he or she will interview. It is very helpful to have a brief summary of the applicant's education, experience, background and interests. Most firms have a list of questions that must be asked of all applicants; it is very useful to draft three to five questions tailor-drafted for the specific applicants.

Listening and observing nonverbal cues are very important in any interview situation, but they are critical in applicant interviewing. In intake and witness interviews the client is paying the firm to provide zealous representation and although some clients may be less than forthcoming with their answers, they probably will answer truthfully because they want their attorney to win the case.

There is a different perspective that should be considered during applicant interviews. The applicant is not paying the attorney and he or she may embellish the truth or omit important critical information because the applicant wants to be hired.

The paralegal must remember that personal questions that do not relate to the employment vacancy are prohibited. Examples of prohibited questions include the following: Are you heterosexual or gay? How many children do you have and/or do you plan to have more children? What religious faith are you? How much do you weigh? For whom did you vote during the last election?

When the interview is complete, the paralegal should, if at all possible, explain to the applicants the next steps in the job selection process and the timeline for the fulfillment of the vacancy.

Additional Interview Terms

- **Curriculum Vitae**: An extensive document that includes an applicant's education and experience as well as personal information normally not found on US resumes. Curriculum vitae are used in the US for fellowships, grants and academic positions.

- **Lead-in:** Information provided by the interviewer on one or more topics asking questions.

- **Panel Interview**: A group of two or more persons usually seated around a conference room table that take turns asking the applicant questions. This tactic allows the firm to save employee time; however, it can create anxiety for applicants.

- **Paraphrase**: this term can be a verb or noun, which refers to the ability to restate someone's statements in the interviewer's own words.

II. ETHICS

As with any other profession, there are rules that govern the ethical behavior of the paralegal/legal assistant profession. In this section, the actual NALA Code has been included. There is also discussion of what each canon means in terms of the actions of paralegals and legal assistants. The Code is directly from the NALA website.

NALA Code of Ethics and Professional Responsibility

Copyright 2007; Adopted 1975; Revised 1979, 1988; 1995; 2007.
National Association of Legal Assistants, Inc.

Each NALA member agrees to follow the canons of the NALA Code of Ethics and Professional Responsibility. Violations of the Code may result in cancellation of membership. First adopted by the NALA membership in May of 1975, the Code of Ethics and Professional Responsibility is the foundation of ethical practices of paralegals in the legal community.

A paralegal must adhere strictly to the accepted standards of legal ethics and to the general principles of proper conduct. The performance of the duties of the paralegal shall be governed by specific canons as defined herein so that justice will be served and goals of the profession attained. (See Model Standards and Guidelines for Utilization of Legal Assistants, Section II.)

The canons of ethics set forth hereafter are adopted by the National Association of Legal Assistants, Inc., as a general guide intended to aid paralegals and attorneys. The enumeration of these rules does not mean there are not others of equal importance although not specifically mentioned. Court rules, agency rules and statutes must be taken into consideration when interpreting the canons.

Definition

Legal assistants, also known as paralegals, are a distinguishable group of persons who assist attorneys in the delivery of legal services. Through formal education, training and experience, legal assistants have knowledge and expertise regarding the legal system and substantive and procedural law which qualify them to do work of a legal nature under the supervision of an attorney.

In 2001, NALA members also adopted the ABA definition of a legal assistant/paralegal, as follows: A legal assistant or paralegal is a person qualified by education, training or work experience who is employed or retained by a lawyer, law office, corporation, governmental agency or other entity who performs specifically delegated substantive legal work for which a lawyer is responsible. (Adopted by the ABA in 1997)

Canon 1

A paralegal must not perform any of the duties that attorneys only may perform nor take any actions that attorneys may not take.

Canon 2

A paralegal may perform any task which is properly delegated and supervised by an attorney, as long as the attorney is ultimately responsible to the client, maintains a direct relationship with the client, and assumes professional responsibility for the work product.

Canon 3

A paralegal must not: (a) engage in, encourage, or contribute to any act which could constitute the unauthorized practice of law; and (b) establish attorney-client relationships, set fees, give legal opinions or advice or represent a client before a court or agency unless so authorized by that court or agency; and (c) engage in conduct or take any action which would assist or involve the attorney in a violation of professional ethics or give the appearance of professional impropriety.

Canon 4

A paralegal must use discretion and professional judgment commensurate with knowledge and experience but must not render independent legal judgment in place of an attorney. The services of an attorney are essential in the public interest whenever such legal judgment is required.

Canon 5

A paralegal must disclose his or her status as a paralegal at the outset of any professional relationship with a client, attorney, a court or administrative agency or personnel thereof, or a member of the general public. A paralegal must act prudently in determining the extent to which a client may be assisted without the presence of an attorney.

Canon 6

A paralegal must strive to maintain integrity and a high degree of competency through education and training with respect to professional responsibility, local rules and practice, and through continuing education in substantive areas of law to better assist the legal profession in fulfilling its duty to provide legal service.

Canon 7

A paralegal must protect the confidences of a client and must not violate any rule or statute now in effect or hereafter enacted controlling the doctrine of privileged communications between a client and an attorney.

Canon 8

A paralegal must disclose to his or her employer or prospective employer any pre-existing client or personal relationship that may conflict with the interests of the employer or prospective employer and/or their clients.

Canon 9

A paralegal must do all other things incidental, necessary, or expedient for the attainment of the ethics and responsibilities as defined by statute or rule of court.

Canon 10

A paralegal's conduct is guided by bar associations' codes of professional responsibility and rules of professional conduct.

Canon 1

This section of the code probably causes more problems for paralegals, legal assistants and non-lawyers in general than all of the other sections combined. Part of the problems that arise from this canon stem from the fact that there is ambiguity as to what type of work is relegated to attorneys only.

A good example of this problem involves the use of paralegals and non-attorneys in Social Security Disability Administrative hearings. Paralegals can represent clients in Social Security administrative matters but cannot represent clients (sometimes the same clients) at other administrative hearings and in court. It can be very frustrating and confusing for non-attorneys to try to remember when they can perform legal work which is akin to attorney work and when they cannot.

Another gray area surrounding Canon 1 is the statement, "take any action that an attorney may not take." The wording of this section causes all kinds of problems because most non-attorneys do not know what actions attorneys cannot take. A paralegal would have to read, understand and become familiar with the Code of Professional Responsibility for the attorneys in his or her state. Once he or she read the attorney code of professional responsibility, he or she would then have to keep abreast of all the changes that are made to the code. This would be a daunting task because the updated info is usually only sent to attorneys. Although it would be difficult for paralegals to access and adhere to the changes, they are still responsible if they break one of the rules even if they were not aware of the change in the rules.

The best advice to paralegals in regards to Canon 1 is to always work under the supervision of a licensed attorney, because any work done without the benefit of attorney supervision can subject the paralegal to violation of canon 1 and charges of unauthorized practice of law.

Canon 2

This gives paralegals more latitude and freedom to perform more substantive work. This canon even allows paralegals to perform work that attorneys normally perform. The key to the increased substantive workload is attorney supervision. A well-trained paralegal can perform most of the work needed to take a case from inception to judgment provided the attorney supervises the paralegal, maintains direct contact with the client and is the person who actually litigates the case in a court of law.

Canon 3

This basically states that a paralegal cannot hold him or herself out as a lawyer; he or she cannot create an attorney-client relationship nor may a paralegal set fees for his or her work. Paralegals routinely get into hot water when they charge clients for filling out divorce and bankruptcy forms for the clients. Although the argument has been made that the paralegals are merely performing clerical work and are not providing legal advice and services, this argument has failed repeatedly. Paralegals who charge clients to fill out forms are in violation of Canons 2 & 3 because they are performing legal work for which they are not supervised and they are charging clients for their services in the same manner that an attorney would so do.

Canon 4

This requires that paralegals exercise professionalism and discernment in all legal matters. However, the canon cautions that a paralegal's experience and judgment cannot be a substitute for an attorney's professional legal services. In essence, even if a paralegal has impeccable judgment and thirty years of experience, he or she is prohibited from providing legal advice that has not been approved by an attorney.

Canon 5

This canon is very important and speaks to the issue of fraudulent misrepresentation. A paralegal must tell all parties involved: clients, court and other attorneys at the *beginning* of any legal matters that he or she is not an attorney. It is easy to apply the "don't ask don't tell" principle here and lots of paralegals have gotten into trouble for doing just that. The long and short of this canon is that a paralegal has a duty to inform any and all persons who might seek their help and/or advice that he or she is not an attorney.

Canon 6

This speaks to the issue of continuing education. This canon states that a paralegal must seek to improve his or her knowledge of the profession and must participate in continuing education courses and training. The rationale behind this principle is that a well-trained paralegal who has up to date knowledge is an asset to the attorney with whom he or she works, and to the legal community and society as a whole. In essence, the more comprehensive and current a paralegal's training, the more he or she is able to help his or her attorney assist clients and provide better access to justice within our society.

Canon 7

This states that although a paralegal is not an attorney, he or she is still bound to maintain the client's confidentiality. Most states include the paralegal in the attorney/client privilege protection afforded attorneys and their clients. This canon also states that a paralegal cannot violate any laws regarding attorney client privilege and communications.

Canon 8

This states that a paralegal is required to inform his or her employer, current clients and potential employers of any information that would represent a possible conflict of interest. This canon is very important since most paralegals work closely with the clients and with their documents, sp a possible conflict of interest can be devastating if discovered during litigation. If there is a potential conflict of interest a "Chinese Wall" or war room can be created that will allow the paralegal to keep her job at the firm while restricting his or her access to the information that would be impacted by the conflict of interest. The ability to create a "Chinese Wall" is contingent upon early notice of a potential conflict of interest.

Canon 9

This merely states that a paralegal must comply with the attainment and maintenance of ethical behavior and integrity in the legal profession.

Canon 10

This canon sums up all of the previous canons by stating that a paralegal is subject to and bound by the attorney code of professional responsibility.

Additional Prohibited Behavior

Although the NALA canons do not address the following scenarios, most people know that the described behavior is unethical for paralegals and attorneys alike. The prohibited specific behaviors are as follows:

- A paralegal cannot accept funds from clients without direct instruction from his or her attorney supervisor.

- A paralegal cannot at any time co-mingle his or her money with the client's money.

- A paralegal cannot enter into or maintain a personal relationship with a former or current client.

- A paralegal cannot engage in activities that would be considered moral turpitude, i.e. adultery, cheating on taxes and gambling.

- A paralegal should not engage in illegal and/or immoral activities: partaking of dangerous street drugs and engaging in illegal sexual activities.

III. LEGAL RESEARCH

The best skill that a paralegal can master is the ability to perform legal research accurately and quickly. In today's world of Lexis, Westlaw and PACER ,most people think of legal research as a quick one button search. However, there are times when even the best databases crash and electrical power is reduced or totally blacked out. What happens when the legal research tools aren't available at the touch of a button?

The purpose of this section is to provide an overview of legal research tools, sources and resources. The skills required to perform legal research via Lexis will be discussed, as well as the skills needed to perform legal research without electronic means, using books, reporters, loose leaf updates and periodicals.

How is legal research accomplished? In the legal world, as in any other discipline or field of education, there are primary, secondary and tertiary sources of information. The source that is usually viewed as most accurate is the primary source because the original information is usually found in this type of resource; the next source is called the secondary source because it directly discusses what was stated in the primary source. The final source is the tertiary source, which is sometimes only tangentially related to the original information.

Primary Authority

The term authority is used in the legal field because the information found will be used to exert "binding, mandatory or persuasive influence over subsequent similar cases." The information found in the primary legal books in a particular state have the power to control the outcome of other states; these primary sources have control or authority over later cases. Some examples of primary legal authority are: the U.S. Constitution, Statutes, Administrative Regulations and decisions from the highest courts in a specified jurisdiction i.e. US. Supreme Court, Kansas Supreme Court or the New Hampshire Court of Appeals.

Secondary and Tertiary Authority

Secondary authority is comprised of: Digests, Citators and Restatements alongside other legal books and databases. Tertiary sources are legal magazines, law review articles, legal journals, legal encyclopedia and legal dictionaries.

Where to Start Researching

So where does one start in order to perform legal research? Well, where one starts is a function of what one already knows. For example if the case number is already known, then it would be prudent to go directly to the case decision in one of the reporters, or to the actual case file if the researcher is located in a municipality that is close to the court file room that houses that case file. However, what happens if a paralegal is given a term that he or she does not know and is asked to find the latest information on the topic? In this case, it would make sense to utilize a tertiary source: a legal dictionary or legal encyclopedia to find the definition of what the topic entails.

For example: a paralegal is tasked with finding the latest development or decision on a case called Lodestar. The paralegal looks up the definition of any words he or she does not know, then researches articles that explain the topic further. These secondary authority resources often list the citation or identifying page numbers of original cases that have provided decisions regarding Lodestar. Usually one case pertaining to the topic will make reference to the primary authority that has addressed the topic that is being researched. In a short while, the paralegal has been able to obtain the definition of the term, find articles regarding the topic and compile a list of recent cases that have dealt with the topic without relying on a database.

Legal research is a skill akin to cooking in that it is good to have all sorts of shortcuts and readymade products, but when it is all said and done, it is essential to provide what is needed even when there are no shortcuts.

Legal Databases

There are few people in the legal field who are unfamiliar with LEXIS, Westlaw and PACER. These are all databases that charge a fee, though there are free legal research resources on the Internet, as well. Some of them are: Findlaw, Justia, Leagle.com, OneCle and Openjurist. There are also reduced fee cites: Scrib'd and others operated by state governments.

Whether research is conducted online or in the law library, paralegals need to know the citation abbreviations for the more commonly used legal resources.

Sources of Legal Information

- American Digest System: refers to the huge, master index of all US case law. This set of reference materials is published by Thomson/West. It is comprised of the Century Digest, the General Digest and the Decennial Digests.

- American Jurisprudence: AmJur is a legal encyclopedia published by West Publishing. Uses the West Key system that allows for cross indexing and searching from encyclopedia to digests to reporters.

- American Law Reports: ALR is a secondary source (group of annotations) that explains the differences in application of legal topics and laws in various jurisdictions. This tool is used in the same manner that one uses the legal encyclopedia because it provides a wealth of information about specific topics; therefore, it is an excellent starting point if a paralegal knows very little about a topic.

- Atlantic Reporter: This is a regional compilation of Supreme Court and appellate cases by West Publishing that covers Maine, New York, New Jersey, the District of Columbia, Maryland, New Hampshire, Connecticut, Delaware, Vermont and Rhode Island.
- Code of Federal Regulations: The definition given for Code of Federal Regulations at http://www.archives.gov/federal-register/cfr/ is: "The Code of Federal Regulations (CFR) is a codification (arrangement of) the general and permanent rules published in the *Federal Register* by the executive departments and agencies of the Federal Government." This legal reference tool is a lifesaver for paralegals who are assigned the task of finding recent executive or administrative decisions, because the CFR is much easier to find information in than the Federal Register. The CFR is arranged into fifty titles that cover various topics and subjects reported in the Federal Register. The CFR is updated annually, but day-to-day changes are reported in the Federal Register.

- Corpus Juris Secondum: The CJS is a legal encyclopedia published by Thomson Reuters. Useful starting point when a paralegal knows very little about a topic.

- Decennial Digest: This tool is part of the American Digest System. These volumes are published to reflect ten years of information.

- Federal Register: The definition given at http://www.archives.gov/federal-register/the-federal-register/ reads as follows: "Published every Federal working day, the *Federal Register* is the official gazette of the United States Government. It provides legal notice of administrative rules, notices and Presidential documents in a comprehensive, uniform manner. The *Federal Register* contains: Federal Agency Regulations, Proposed Rules and Public Notices, Executive Orders, Proclamations, Other Presidential Documents." This is a comprehensive reference tool that will provide the paralegal with up to date information on all actions taken in the legal arena with the exception of actual court decisions. The major drawback to the Federal Register in terms of research is that it the entries are not codified. Since it is published daily, there is often a one-day lag in information.

- Federal Reporter Third Edition: This is a federal case law compilation published by West that covers cases from 1993 to the present. It uses the West key system. There were two previous editions: F, which covered cases from 1880 to 1924 and F2d, which covered cases from 1924 to 1993.

- Federal Supplement, Second Series This is a Federal compilation of District court cases published by West that also uses the West key system. The series covers cases from 1998 to present. The previous series covered cases from 1933 to 1998.

- Northeastern Reporter: Published by West, the Northeastern Reporter is part of the National Reporter system. The reporter covers US state appellate case law from the following states: Illinois, Indiana, Massachusetts, New York and Ohio. There have been two series of North Eastern Reporters: the first series covered cases from 1884 to 1936 and the second series N.E. 2d covered from 1936 to present time. This reference tool uses the West key number system.

- Northwestern Reporter: This is published by West as part of the National Reporter System. This reporter series provided appellate case decisions for the following states: Iowa, Michigan, Minnesota, Nebraska, North Dakota, South Dakota and Wisconsin. The Northwestern reporter also uses the West key number system. There have been two series for the reporter: NW, which covered cases from 1879-1941 and NW2d, which covers cases from 1942 to present.

- Shepard's Citations: This is a legal research source called a citatory that provides a complete and comprehensive list of all cases that have mentioned or cited a particular case. This is the ultimate legal research tool, because using Shepard's (or Shepardizing) is the most accurate way to determine if a case is still "good law". In Shepard's citators, cases are denoted as being vacated, dismissed, followed, criticized, overturned, abrogated, and distinguished. These terms are referred to as treatment of the case and letters are used to denote the treatment i.e.: v= vacated, f= followed. The Shepard method of researching case law was started by John Shepard in the 1870's. The method has been adopted and improved by legal research giants Lexis and Westlaw. Although most Shepardizing is now done online some law libraries still maintain the hard copy Shepard's citators.

- US Code: USC the definition provided by http://uscode.house.gov/search/criteria.shtml reads as follows: "The United States Code is a consolidation and codification by subject matter of the general and permanent laws of the United States. It is prepared by the Office of the Law Revision Counsel of the United States House of Representatives." There are two other unofficial reporters that contain the US Code, the United States Code Annotated (USCA) and the United States Code Service (USCS). The US code is divided into 51 titles and has chapters, subchapters and sections.

- US Supreme Court Reports: Published by the US Government Printing Office (GPO), this is the official reporter of the decisions of the Supreme Court. There are two other unofficial reporters: the Supreme Court Reporter (S.Ct) and the Supreme Court Reports Lawyers Edition (L.Ed.)

Once the paralegal has mastered the art of finding a case, then comes the task of reading the cases and deciding whether or not they are beneficial to the issue. One of the first things that a paralegal must know when he or she looks at cases are the components of the decision or opinion.

The first page of the decision will have the caption or citation information. This information is comprised of the names of the parties, the volume and page information of the case, the date the case was argued and decided, the names of the judges and the attorneys. There should also be a brief summary of the issues decided as well as a brief summary of the holding. Decisions reported on Lexis have head notes and West reporters have the key system. If a paralegal learns to look at the head notes, brief issue and holding summaries first, he or she can save a lot of time. The advent of Lexis and Westlaw shortened the case reading and analysis time tremendously. Only the cases that have issues and holdings favorable to your case are relevant to the first review. Later, as the paralegal is helping the attorney plan his or her strategy, the paralegal will want to have a list or printout of cases that the opposing side will probably use in their case.

Latin Legal Terms

There are hundreds of Latin legal terms that have been used in courts of law for centuries. In the US, most courts have reduced the number of Latin legal terms that are still in use today. However, there are terms that you still need to memorize. The paralegal can increase his or her mastery of the terms by consulting a copy of *Duhaime's Dictionary of Latin Law Maxims and Terms*. Several of the more commonly used terms and their meanings here are directly from the Duhaime Dictionary.

Terms and Definitions

Ab Initio
Latin: from the start; from the beginning.

Actus Dei Nemini Facit Injuriam
Latin: An act of God causes legal injury to no one.

Actus Regis Nemini Est Damnosa
Latin: The law will not work a wrong.

Actus Reus
Latin: a prohibited act.

Ad Hoc
Latin: limited in time; to this point.

Ad Infinitum
Latin: forever; without limit; indefinitely.

Ad Litem
Latin: for the suit.

Amicus Curiae
Latin: friend of the court.

Animus
Latin: intention.

Animus Contrahendi
Latin: an intention to contract.

Animus Furandi

Latin: an intent to do wrong.

Bona Fide

Latin: good faith.

Bona Vacantia

Property that belongs to no person, and which may be claimed by a finder.

Boni Judicis Est Ampliare Jurisdictionem

Latin: good justice is broad jurisdiction.

Causa Causans

The real, effective cause of damage.

Causa Proxima Et Non Remota Spectatur

Latin: the immediate, not the remote cause, is to be considered.

Causa Sine Qua Non

An intervening cause of loss which, though not direct, may nonetheless contribute to the loss.

Caveat

Latin: let him beware. A formal warning.

Contemporanea Expositio

That the meaning of words in a document are to be understood in the sense which they bore at the time of the document.

Corpus Delicti

Latin: the body of the offense.

De Facto

Latin: in fact.

De Fide et Officio Judicis non Recipitur Quaestio, sed de Scientia Sive sit Eror Juris sive Facti

Latin: The bona fides and honesty of purpose of a judge cannot be questioned, but his decision may be impugned for error of law or of fact.

De injuria sua propria absque tali causa

Latin: of his own wrong (or injury) without any other cause.

De Jure
Latin: of the law.

De Non Sane Memorie
Latin: of insane memory.

De Novo
Latin: new.

Dicta or Dictum
Latin: saying.

Dies Dominicus Non Est Juridicus
Latin: Sunday is not a day for judicial or legal proceedings.

Donatio Mortis Causa
A death-bed gift, made by a dying person, with the intent that the person receiving the gift shall keep the thing if death ensues.

Duces Tecum
Latin: bring with you.

Dum Casta
Latin: for so long as she remains chaste.

En banc
(French) As a full bench.

Error In Objecto
A mistake by a perpetrator as to the identity of the victim; an error as to the object of his act.

Erunt animae duae in carne una
Latin: two souls in one flesh.

Ex Parte
Latin: outside the awareness of a party; for one party only.

Ex Patriate
A person who has abandoned his or her country of origin and citizenship and has become a subject or citizen of another country.

Ex Post Facto

Latin: after the fact.

Furtum

Latin: theft or a thing stolen.

Habeas Corpus

Latin: a court petition which orders that a person being detained be produced before a judge for a hearing to decide whether the detention is lawful.

Hereditas

Latin: the estate of a deceased person.

Hereditas Damnosa

Latin: an inheritance that is more of a burden than a benefit.

Ignorantia Juris Non Excusat

Latin: ignorance of the law is no excuse.

In Absentia

Latin: in the absence of.

In Camera

A closed and private session of Court or some other deliberating body.

In Fictione Juris Semper Aequitas Existit

Latin: With legal fictions, equity always exists.

In haec verba

Latin: verbatim.

In Jure Non Remota Causa Sed Proxima Spectatur

Latin: In law the near cause is looked to, not the remote one.

In Limine

Latin: at the beginning or on the threshold.

In Loco Parentis

A person who, though not the natural parent, has acted as a parent to a child and may thus be liable to legal obligations as if he/she were a natural parent.

In Pari Delicto
Latin: both parties are equally at fault.

In Personam
Latin: regarding a person; a right, action, judgment or entitlement that is attached to a specific person(s).

In Rem
Latin: regarding a thing; proprietary in nature; a right or judgment related to the use or ownership of an item of property.

Inter Alia
Latin: 'among other things', 'for example' or 'including'.

Inter Vivos
Latin: from one living person to another living person.

In tota fine erga omnes et omnia
Latin: for all purposes, in regards to all and everything.

In Toto
Latin: in total.

Intuitu Personae
Latin: Because of the person.

Ipso facto
Latin: By the act itself.

Ipso jure
Latin: by operation of law.

Malum in se
Latin: something wrong in itself.

Malum prohibitum
Latin: wrong because prohibited.

Mandamus
A writ which commands an individual, organization (eg. government), administrative tribunal or court to perform a certain action, usually to correct a prior illegal action or a failure to act in the first place.

Mansuetae Naturae

Latin: animals which are now generally domestic, presumed gentle and readily tamed, such as dogs, cats, cows and horses.

Mea Culpa

Latin: I am guilty.

Mens Rea

Latin for guilty mind; guilty knowledge or intention to commit a prohibited act.

Mobilia Sequuntur Personam, Immobilia Situa

Latin: movables follow the person, immovables their locality.

Modus Operandi

Latin: method of operation.

Nisi Prius

Latin: unless, before. More commonly, a civil jury trial.

Nolle Prosequi

Latin: no prosecution.

Nolo Contendere

Latin: I will not defend.

Non Compos Mentis

Latin: Not of sound mind.

Non Est Factum

Latin: not his deed.

Non Sequitur

Latin: it does not follow.

Noscitur a sociis

Latin: that the meaning of a word may be known from accompanying words.

Nota Bene

Latin: note well

Pendente Lite
Latin: during litigation.

Per Capita
Latin: by the head.

Per Curiam
Latin: on behalf of the court.

Per Incuriam
Latin: through want of care.

Per Infortunium
Latin: by misadventure.

Per Quod Consortium Amisit
Latin: whereby he loses the company of his wife.

Per Se
Latin: of itself.

Præcipe or Precipe
Latin: an initiating document presented to a court clerk to be officially issued on behalf of the court or a the covering memo or letter from the lawyer (or plaintiff) which accompanies and formally asks for the writ to be issued by the court officer.

Praemunire
An offence initially to prefer the Pope or his authority as against the King of England or Parliament, but later included a wide assortment of offenses against the King and always leading to serious penalties.

Precarium
Latin: the giving of land as a reward or to secure a debt.

Prima Facie
(Latin) A legal presumption which means on the face of it or at first sight.

Pro Bono
Latin: for the good.

Pro Forma
Latin: for the sake of form.

Pro Rata
Latin: to divide proportionate to a certain rate or interest.

Pro Se
Latin: on one's own behalf.

Pro Socio
Latin: on behalf of a partnership.

Pro Tempore
Latin: something done temporarily only and not intended to be permanent.

Quaere
Latin for "query" as in an issue on which some doubt or question exists.

Quantum Meruit
Latin: as much as is deserved.

Quia Emptores
A 1290 English statute that held that notwithstanding the subdivision (subinfeudation) of a feeholding; the new tenant owed feudal rights and obligations not to the seller but to the Land Lord.

Quicquid Plantatur Solo, Solo Cedit
Latin: whatever is planted in the ground, belongs to the ground.

Quid Pro Quo
Latin: something for something.

Qui Facit Per Alium Facit Per Se
Latin: he who acts through another, acts himself.

Res Derelicta
Latin: a thing abandoned.

Res Gestae
Latin: things done.

Res Ipsa Loquitur
Latin: the thing speaks for itself.

Res Judicata
Latin: already subject to judicial determination.

Res Noviter Veniens Ad Notitiam
Latin: Fact(s) newly coming to knowledge.

Respondeat superior
Latin: let the principal answer.

Sine Die
Latin: without a day. Taken to mean without fixing a day for continuation.

Sine Qua Non
Latin: without which, not.

Situs
Latin: location.

Stare Decisis
Latin: stay with what has been decided.

Sub Judice
Latin: under judicial consideration.

Subpoena
Latin: an order of a court which requires a person to be present at a certain time and place or suffer a penalty (subpoena means, literally, under penalty).

Sui Generis
Latin: of its own kind.

Sui Juris
Latin: one's own law; having full capacity.

Ultra Petita
Latin: beyond that which is sought.

Ultra Vires
Latin: beyond the powers.

Use
Latin: trust.

Usufruct
The rights to the product of another's property.

Usury

Excessive or illegal interest rate.

IV. SUBSTANTIVE LAW

The American Legal System

In order to understand today's laws and decisions, one must first understand the American Legal system and how it came into being.

Federal government and individual state governments came about as a result of the US Constitution. It should be noted that the United States Constitution, created in 1787, is the oldest constitution in the world still in use. Unlike many other countries, we have added only 27 amendments to the US Constitution in 226 years.

After the colonies declared their independence in 1776, the leaders of the new country decided that we needed a defining document that would state how we should be governed. The delegates met for over four months (May – September 1787) in Philadelphia in what was called the Constitutional Convention. On September 17, 1787 the group had a formal constitution that had to be ratified by the states. The Constitution was ratified in 1789 and the American Legal System was born.

The new Constitution, which laid the framework as to state and Federal governmental powers as well as the requirements for government officers, was made up of eight articles. The constitution set out the rights and responsibilities of the citizens as well as for the governing bodies.

The Bill of Rights

In addition to the articles, there are amendments as well. The first ten amendments are called the Bill of Rights. These ten amendments are as follows:

1. Congress shall make no law respecting an establishment of religion, or prohibiting the free exercise thereof; or abridging the freedom of speech, or of the press; or the right of the people peaceably to assemble, and to petition the Government for a redress of grievances.

2. A well regulated Militia, being necessary to the security of a free State, the right of the people to keep and bear Arms, shall not be infringed.

3. No Soldier shall, in time of peace be quartered in any house, without the consent of the Owner, nor in time of war, but in a manner to be prescribed by law.

4. The right of the people to be secure in their persons, houses, papers, and effects, against unreasonable searches and seizures, shall not be violated, and no Warrants shall issue, but upon probable cause, supported by Oath or affirmation, and particularly describing the place to be searched, and the persons or things to be seized.

5. No person shall be held to answer for a capital, or otherwise infamous crime, unless on a presentment or indictment of a Grand Jury, except in cases arising in the land or naval forces, or in the Militia, when in actual service in time of War or public danger; nor shall any person be subject for the same offence to be twice put in jeopardy of life or limb; nor shall be compelled in any criminal case to be a witness against himself, nor be deprived of life, liberty, or property, without due process of law; nor shall private property be taken for public use, without just compensation.

6. In all criminal prosecutions, the accused shall enjoy the right to a speedy and public trial, by an impartial jury of the State and district wherein the crime shall have been committed, which district shall have been previously ascertained by law, and to be informed of the nature and cause of the accusation; to be confronted with the witnesses against him; to have compulsory process for obtaining witnesses in his favor, and to have the Assistance of Counsel for his defence.

7. In suits at common law, where the value in controversy shall exceed twenty dollars, the right of trial by jury shall be preserved, and no fact tried by a jury, shall be otherwise re-examined in any court of the United States, than according to the rules of the common law.

8. Excessive bail shall not be required, nor excessive fines imposed, nor cruel and unusual punishments inflicted.

9. The enumeration in the Constitution, of certain rights, shall not be construed to deny or disparage others retained by the people.

10. The powers not delegated to the United States by the Constitution, nor prohibited by it to the States, are reserved to the States respectively, or to the people.

Branches of Government

The Constitution provided for three branches of government:

- The executive branch, which is made up of the President of the United States, each state's governor and the Administrative agencies' chief executives.
- The legislative branch, which consists of the US Congress and the state legislative bodies of each state. The Senate and the House of Representatives make up the Congress.
- The judicial branch is comprised of the US Supreme Court, the Federal courts and the state courts.

Each one of the branches of the government acts as checks and balances for the other branches and each has a very important and unique task in the operation of the Federal Government.

For most paralegals and other legal personnel, the branch of government that holds the most significance in their daily work lives is the judicial branch. The judicial branch is assigned the task of enforcing the laws made at the Federal, state, county and local levels.

The Supreme Court

The highest court in the judicial system is the US Supreme Court, which consists of one Chief Justice and eight other justices. Supreme Court justices are nominated by the President, approved by the Senate and serve for life. They can retire if they desire but they cannot be removed from office except in extreme circumstances, and they do not run in elections.

The seminal case *Marbury v. Madison*, decided in 1803, established the doctrine of judicial review. The first woman to be appointed to the Supreme Court was Justice Sandra Day O'Connor and the first African American Justice to serve was Justice Thurmond Marshall. At the present time there are three women on the Supreme Court, one African American justice and one Hispanic justice.

The Supreme Court has been a strong force in shaping public policy and American society. In 1954, the Supreme Court denounced segregation in schools as a result of the *Brown v. Board of Education* case. In 1967 the Supreme Court abolished miscegenation and interracial marriage prohibition laws in *Loving v. Virginia*. The Court established the right to use birth control in *Griswold v. Connecticut* in 1965 and in 1973 the Court gave women the right to obtain legal abortions in the *Roe v. Wade* case. There are hundreds of other Supreme Court cases that have had a tremendous impact of the lives of Americans, some of which were not as well publicized as the previously named cases.

How does a case get to the Supreme Court? At some point, everyone has heard a disgruntled litigant state that they intend to take a case all the way to the Supreme Court, but can he or she really do that? The answer to that query lies within the pages of the Constitution and the answer is, "yes and no."

The answer is "yes" regarding taking a case all the way to the Supreme Court if the case falls under Article Three of the Constitution. Article Three of the Constitution states "In all cases affecting ambassadors, other public Ministers and Consuls, and those in which a State shall be a party, the Supreme Court shall have original jurisdiction." If a person falls under any of these categories, their case must be heard by the highest court in the land.

The answer to the question can be "no" if the case is not covered by Article Three because in this Article the framers stated "In all other cases before mentioned the Supreme Court shall have appellate jurisdiction both as to law and fact, with such exceptions and under regulations as the Congress shall make." The meaning behind this statement is that the Supreme Court will function as an appellate court and can at its discretion decide which cases it will and will not hear during a session. Any person or entity that would like to have the Supreme Court hear his or her appellate case must file what is known as petition for a writ of certiorari and the Supreme Court can use its discretion as to whether it will grant or deny certiorari. Four of the nine justices must vote to hear the case in order for the writ of certiorari to be granted. According to the statistics kept and cited at http://www.uscourts.gov/educational-resources/get-informed/supreme-court/supreme-court-procedures.aspx, only 100-150 of the 7,000 cases submitted for review are heard by the Supreme court each year. "The Court usually is not under any obligation to hear these cases, and it usually only does so if the case could have national significance, might harmonize conflicting decisions in the federal Circuit courts, and/or could have precedential value."

If the US Supreme Court declines to hear an appeal, the appellant has no further recourse because there is no other court to which a complaint about the Supreme Court can be made.

Constitutional Clauses

There are hundreds of clauses within the United States Constitution and they all serve a very important purpose. However, there are several clauses that are more frequently applied and are therefore better known to the general population.

The Preamble

The first clause is the Preamble to the Constitution. At one time, every American school child was required to learn the Preamble to the US Constitution; even though that requirement no longer applies, it is incumbent upon every legal student to know the Preamble because it tells the purpose of the Constitution. The Preamble reads as follows:

"We the people of the United States, in order to form a more perfect union, establish justice, insure domestic tranquility, provide for the common defense, promote the general welfare, and secure the blessings of liberty to ourselves and our posterity, do ordain and establish this Constitution for the United States of America".

This simple statement has maintained order and controlled the United States for more than 226 years. Although this Preamble is a basic concept and not by any means elaborate or even complicated, it represents the sentiments of the framers and the purpose of the entire document. It is not known whether the framers realized the magnitude of the document they were creating nor if they had an inkling of its longevity, but it is now acknowledged that the US Constitution is the oldest document of its kind still in use in the world today.

The Commerce Clause

The next very familiar clause in the Constitution is the Commerce Clause. The Commerce Clause in Article 1, Section 8 reads as follows:

"The Congress shall have Power To lay and collect Taxes, Duties, Imposts and Excises, to pay the Debts and provide for the common Defence and general Welfare of the United States; but all Duties, Imposts and Excises shall be uniform throughout the United States;

To borrow money on the credit of the United States;

To regulate Commerce with foreign Nations, and among the several States, and with the Indian Tribes;

To establish an uniform Rule of Naturalization, and uniform Laws on the subject of Bankruptcies throughout the United States;

To coin Money, regulate the Value thereof, and of foreign Coin, and fix the Standard of Weights and Measures;

To provide for the Punishment of counterfeiting the Securities and current Coin of the United States;

To establish Post Offices and Post Roads;

To promote the Progress of Science and useful Arts, by securing for limited Times to Authors and Inventors the exclusive Right to their respective Writings and Discoveries;

To constitute Tribunals inferior to the Supreme Court;

To define and punish Piracies and Felonies committed on the high Seas, and Offenses against the Law of Nations;

To declare War, grant Letters of Marque and Reprisal, and make Rules concerning Captures on Land and Water;

To raise and support Armies, but no Appropriation of Money to that Use shall be for a longer Term than two Years;

To provide and maintain a Navy;

To make Rules for the Government and Regulation of the land and naval Forces;

To provide for calling forth the Militia to execute the Laws of the Union, suppress Insurrections and repel Invasions;

To provide for organizing, arming, and disciplining, the Militia, and for governing such Part of them as may be employed in the Service of the United States, reserving to the States respectively, the Appointment of the Officers, and the Authority of training the Militia according to the discipline prescribed by Congress;

To exercise exclusive Legislation in all Cases whatsoever, over such District (not exceeding ten Miles square) as may, by Cession of particular States, and the acceptance of Congress, become the Seat of the Government of the United States, and to exercise like Authority over all Places purchased by the Consent of the Legislature of the State in which the Same shall be, for the Erection of Forts, Magazines, Arsenals, dock-Yards, and other needful Buildings; And

To make all Laws which shall be necessary and proper for carrying into Execution the foregoing Powers, and all other Powers vested by this Constitution in the Government of the United States, or in any Department or Officer thereof."

Although Section 8 of Article 1 covers a lot of territory, it places emphasis on the concept of the US government's authority to regulate commerce between states and with foreign nations, to borrow money on the credit of the United States and the authority to coin money and to collect taxes. The Constitution provided for actions that mystify the modern population that has not taken the time to read and understand the Constitution. A lot of complaint is made regarding the US government trading with and borrowing from foreign countries, but the framers of the Constitution provided authority for such actions. The words that they wrote still are binding and effective for the problems the nation faces today. The Commerce Clause has been creatively used to abolish discrimination in business that are involved in or affect "the interstate stream of commerce". The Commerce Clause states that the Congress has the power "To regulate Commerce with foreign Nations, and among the several States, and with the Indian Tribes." Therefore, if a business in California sells, makes or obtains anything from another state, it is involved in interstate commerce and thus subject to Congress' authority.

The Supremacy Clause

The next very familiar clause is the Supremacy Clause. The Supremacy Clause found in Article 6, Section 2 reads as follows:

"All Debts contracted and Engagements entered into, before the Adoption of this Constitution, shall be as valid against the United States under this Constitution, as under the Confederation.

This Constitution, and the Laws of the United States which shall be made in Pursuance thereof; and all Treaties made, or which shall be made, under the Authority of the United States, shall be the supreme Law of the Land; and the Judges in every State shall be bound thereby, any Thing in the Constitution or Laws of any State to the Contrary notwithstanding.

The Senators and Representatives before mentioned, and the Members of the several State Legislatures, and all executive and judicial Officers, both of the United States and of the several States, shall be bound by Oath or Affirmation, to support this Constitution; but no religious Test shall ever be required as a Qualification to any Office or public Trust under the United States."

Although this clause is much shorter than the Commerce Clause, it nevertheless wields a tremendous amount of authority. This clause establishes that the US Constitution, federal statutes, and U.S. treaties are "the supreme law of the land." What this means that in the event that a dispute should arise between a state law and a Federal law, all state judges must follow the Federal law if it is in accordance with the powers granted by the Constitution. The power of the Supremacy Clause has been on display many times in the last century. States have enacted laws or state judges have rendered decisions only to have them set aside because the state laws conflicted with the Federal laws.

The Supremacy Clause is very similar to and is reinforced by the Fourteenth amendment which states: *"No State shall make or enforce any law which shall abridge the privileges or immunities of citizens of the United States."* The Fourteenth Amendment's focus is on the government's relationship with US citizens. However, the idea is still similar. The States cannot make laws that are in conflict with Federal laws that are already in place.

Due Process Clause

The Due Process Clause, explained in Amendment 5 and in Amendment 14, is a clause frequently mentioned in modern times.

The Due Process Clause explained in Amendment 14, section 1 reads:

"1. All persons born or naturalized in the United States, and subject to the jurisdiction thereof, are citizens of the United States and of the State wherein they reside. No State shall make or enforce any law which shall abridge the privileges or immunities of citizens of the United States; nor shall any State deprive any person of life, liberty, or property, without due process of law; nor deny to any person within its jurisdiction the equal protection of the laws.

2. Representatives shall be apportioned among the several States according to their respective numbers, counting the whole number of persons in each State, excluding Indians not taxed. But when the right to vote at any election for the choice of electors for President and Vice-President of the United States, Representatives in Congress, the Executive and Judicial officers of a State, or the members of the Legislature thereof, is denied to any of the male inhabitants of such State, being twenty-one years of age, and citizens of the United States, or in any way abridged, except for participation in rebellion, or other crime, the basis of representation therein shall be reduced in the proportion which the number of such male citizens shall bear to the whole number of male citizens twenty-one years of age in such State.

3. No person shall be a Senator or Representative in Congress, or elector of President and Vice-President, or hold any office, civil or military, under the United States, or under any State, who, having previously taken an oath, as a member of Congress, or as an officer of the United States, or as a member of any State legislature, or as an executive or judicial officer of any State, to support the Constitution of the United States, shall have engaged in insurrection or rebellion against the same, or given aid or comfort to the enemies thereof. But Congress may by a vote of two-thirds of each House, remove such disability.

4. The validity of the public debt of the United States, authorized by law, including debts incurred for payment of pensions and bounties for services in suppressing insurrection or rebellion, shall not be questioned. But neither the United States nor any State shall assume or pay any debt or obligation

incurred in aid of insurrection or rebellion against the United States, or any claim for the loss or emancipation of any slave; but all such debts, obligations and claims shall be held illegal and void.

5. The Congress shall have power to enforce, by appropriate legislation, the provisions of this article."

Both of these amendments specifically state that US citizens must receive due process before they can be deprived of their lives, liberty, or properties. The main concept here is Due Process. What constitutes Due Process? The Merriam Webster Dictionary defines Due Process as: "a course of formal proceedings (as legal proceedings) carried out regularly and in accordance with established rules and principles."

After reading the definition of Due Process and reviewing the wording used in Amendment 5 and Amendment 14 of the Constitution, it becomes clear the framers strongly believed that the citizens were entitled to a trail or some type of formal, legal process before their property could be seized or their freedom and or life taken away from them. The Due Process Clause provides that a fair and equitable hearing in which the citizen can participate be held before anything of value is taken from them. Until 2002, US Citizens were assured that their property would not be seized until there was a legal hearing regarding the seizure that clearly explained the reason and purpose for the intended seizure. This hearing as provided for by the Constitution was conducted before the seizure or deprivation of the property, liberty or life. The framers of the Constitution set up a formula for justice that, if followed, would allow for equitable treatment of all citizens in relation to their property, freedom and lives.

The Establishment Clause

The Establishment Clause set out in the First Amendment is probably the most litigated of all of the Constitutional Clauses. The Establishment Clause says:

"Congress shall make no law respecting an establishment of religion, or prohibiting the free exercise thereof; or abridging the freedom of speech, or of the press; or the right of the people peaceably to assemble, and to petition the Government for a redress of grievance."

Every year the US Supreme Court (as are other Courts of Appeals) is inundated with cases alleging violations of the Establishment Clause. Freedom of Speech litigation is big business in the United States. The United States was founded upon the tenets of freedom of religion, freedom of speech and freedom of the press, so it is understandable that any attempt to influence, censor or regulate these basic rights will be met with resistance. However, although US Citizens enjoy the basic rights provided under the Establishment Clause of the First Amendment, the rights are not absolute. The framers of the Establishment clause wanted the US citizens to liberally enjoy their rights but they also wanted those rights to be tempered by common sense and respect.

Due Process

The Merriam Webster dictionary defines due process as "a course of formal proceedings (as legal proceedings) carried out regularly and in accordance with established rules and principles."

This definition is for procedural due process. There is another definition given by Merriam Webster for the second type of due process:

"A judicial requirement that enacted laws may not contain provisions that result in the unfair, arbitrary, or unreasonable treatment of an individual." This type of due process is called substantive due process.

Why are there two types of due process, and what is the difference?

The concept of due process originated in English Common law, with the Magna Carta (signed in 1215.) That document contained a phrase stating, "No free man shall be seized, or imprisoned ... except by the lawful judgment of his peers, or by the law of the land." Due process is not a new concept!

There are two types of law: procedural and substantive law and hence there are two types of due process. Substantive law speaks to the "meat" of cases. The restriction or deprivation of fundamental rights is paramount in any analysis of substantive due process matters. Substantive law is concerned with actual actions, not the process related to the treatment of the actions or allegations. For example: A state's seizure of a suspected drug dealer's car involves substantive due process. The person may or may not be a drug dealer, but his or her property should not be seized without some type of trial, hearing or formal legal process. In the United States, a citizen is presumed innocent until proven guilty and if that principle holds, the risk of seizing an innocent person's property is significantly reduced.

Procedural law is not centered on the fundamental right or a specific concept, but rather the actions taken that deprive a citizen of his rights. Procedural due process is focused around the procedures or actions required to deprive a person of his rights. For example, a U.S.-born terrorist is still entitled to procedural due process. He or she must still receive notice of the charges against him or her. Even if this terrorist was receiving Social Security, he or she would be entitled to notice of impending termination of his or her benefits in accordance with the procedural safeguards of procedural due process. There are, at the present time, convicted killers serving life sentences who are entitled to compensatory education because their former school system violated their procedural due process rights.

There is a great deal of controversy surrounding the concept of Substantive and Procedural due process but the framers explicitly provided for both, so any changes to either would require a constitutional amendment.

Jurisdiction

The term jurisdiction is used repeatedly every day, and there are several meanings for jurisdiction. For legal purposes according to Black's Law Dictionary jurisdiction is defined as:

"The power and authority constitutionally conferred upon (or constitutionally recognized as existing in) a court or judge to pronounce the sentence of the law, or to award the remedies provided by law, upon a state of facts, proved or ad-mitted, referred to the tribunal for decision, and authorized by law to be the subject of investigation or action by that tribunal, and in favor of or against persons (or a res) who present themselves, or who are brought, before the court in some manner sanctioned by law as proper and sufficient."

This definition is quite comprehensive, but what jurisdiction means for most laypeople is whether or not a court can hear a case. It is a simple matter of not taking your divorce papers to the landlord tenant court to file because landlord tenant judges can't decide divorce cases.

The first matter that should be considered in deciding jurisdiction is whether the court has original or appellate jurisdiction. A plaintiff can file suit in or originate a case in a case of original jurisdiction but cannot do so in a court of appellate jurisdiction. Original jurisdiction courts are the trial-level courts. Small claims, Municipal, Landlord Tenant, circuit and most US district courts are all original jurisdiction courts.

The Supreme Court and the Courts of Appeals have appellate jurisdiction, which means they can only hear cases that originated in a lower court. Appellate courts cannot hear newly filed matters, only those that were decided elsewhere and then sent to them on appeal. The exception to this rule is the US Supreme Court, which has original jurisdiction on matters enumerated in Article Three of the US Constitution: cases affecting Ambassadors, ministers and consuls, disputes between two state governments, between the government and foreign governments and cases in which the state will be a party. Whereas the courts of original jurisdiction can hear a variety of cases, courts of appellate jurisdiction are deemed to have "limited jurisdiction."

Once original jurisdiction is established, another matter that needs to be addressed is the issue of subject matter jurisdiction. Subject matter jurisdiction is defined by the Law department of Cornell University as "...the requirement that the court have power to hear the specific kind of claim that is brought to that court. While the parties may waive personal jurisdiction and submit to the authority of the court, the parties may not waive subject-matter jurisdiction. In fact, the court may dismiss the case *sua sponte* — or, on its own — for lack of subject-matter jurisdiction."

It makes sense to have judges who are familiar with the type of law or subject matter hear the case rather than those who are not. People don't see an eye doctor for open heart surgery. There are, however, a vast majority of state courts that are referred to as courts of general subject matter jurisdiction. These general subject matter courts can hear any Federal and state matters except those that exclusively fall under the jurisdiction of the Federal courts. According to USLegal.com, the state courts are further separated or categorized:

"In state court systems, different courts generally have boundaries set on their subject matter jurisdiction and in every state, one state court or another has subject matter jurisdiction over any controversy that can be heard in courts of that state." Some courts specialize in a particular area of the law, such as probate law, family law, or juvenile law."

There are a few exceptions to subject matter jurisdiction in Federal cases. One exception involves the concept of ancillary jurisdiction. The Federal Practice Manual published by The Sargent Shriver National Center on Poverty Law provides a historical perspective on ancillary jurisdiction:

"The related doctrine of ancillary jurisdiction developed to empower a federal court to hear some counterclaims and third-party claims over which it lacked an independent jurisdictional base. In a case in which a plaintiff filed a federal claim against a defendant, under what circumstances may the defendant bring claims against the plaintiff or others over which there is no independent basis of subject matter jurisdiction? Such claims are brought by defending parties which have not chosen the federal forum. Generally, when a claim bore a logical relationship to the main claim or arose out of the same transaction or occurrence, courts permitted ancillary jurisdiction. Ancillary jurisdiction consequently extended to compulsory counterclaims, cross-claims, and additional parties to such claims. It did not generally extend to permissive counterclaims, which, by definition, lacked the required factual nexus with the main claim."

In essence ancillary jurisdiction allows a court to hear a case that is outside the court's subject matter jurisdiction if there is a second closely related claim that would fall within the court's subject matter jurisdiction.

There is also the issue of personal jurisdiction. Personal jurisdiction is defined by the Legal Information Institute as

"...the power of a court over the parties in the case. Before a court can exercise power over a party, the constitution requires that the party have certain minimum contacts with the forum in which the court sits."

What constitutes "minimum contacts?" The concept does not have to be considered if the defendant resides within the state or resided within the state at the time that the alleged action took place. It becomes a little more difficult to establish minimum contacts if the defendant does not reside in the state or never resided within the state. Long arm statutes are invaluable in these cases, but if long arm statutes are not available then the test for minimum contacts must be applied.

The minimum contact test articulated in *International Shoe Co. v. Washington*, 326 U.S. 310 (1945) is as follows:

"1. Activities of non-resident are systematic and continuous for a substantial period of time. 2. Defendant enjoys the benefits and protections of the forum state and can resort to forum state's courts for enforcement of its rights 3. Minimum contacts connected to action that gives rise to harm – ensures fair and orderly administration of laws 4. Once minimum contacts are established, court will look to Plaintiff and Defendant's burdens and interest of adjudication to maintain fairness. 5. Place of Domicile: Defendant's physical presence +and a manifested intent to remain establishes minimum contacts."

Personal jurisdiction can also be obtained by consent or through tag jurisdiction. Tag or transient jurisdiction as defined by USLegal.com is:

"Personal jurisdiction over a defendant who is served with process while in the forum state only temporarily such as during travel. Transient jurisdiction is based on service within the forum of a nonresident defendant passing through the state, and has been upheld by the Supreme Court in Burnham v. Superior Court of Cal., 495 U.S. 604 (U.S. 1990). "

A few other terms that need mentioning in connection with jurisdiction are: pendent jurisdiction which is similar to ancillary jurisdiction, supplemental jurisdiction, In Rem jurisdiction and Quasi In Rem jurisdiction. Pendent jurisdiction is defined by the Free Legal Dictionary as

"The discretionary power of a federal court to permit the assertion of a related state law claim, along with a federal claim between the same parties, properly before the court, provided that the federal claim and the state law claim derive from the same set of facts."

Supplemental jurisdiction is defined by the Legal Information Institute as:

"A way for federal courts to hear claims for which they would not ordinarily have jurisdiction. Supplemental jurisdiction only exists in the situation where a lawsuit consists of more than one claim, and the federal court has valid jurisdiction (either diversity jurisdiction or federal question jurisdiction) over at least one of the claims."

The Free Legal Dictionary defines In Rem and Quasi In Rem jurisdiction as:

"The power of a court to hear a case and enforce a judgment against a party, even if the party is not personally before the court, solely because the party has an interest in real property or Personal Property within the geographical limits of the court...Both in rem and quasi in rem jurisdiction are based on the presence of the party's property within the court's territorial authority. In each instance the court may exercise jurisdiction without the actual presence of the party in court. The distinction between the two types of jurisdiction involves the nature of the dispute to which each applies and the extent of the authority each conveys.

In rem (Latin for "against the thing") jurisdiction applies where the dispute involves the property itself. A court exercising in rem jurisdiction has the authority to make a decision as to the property's ownership that will be binding on all the world. Quasi in rem (Latin for "sort of against the thing") jurisdiction applies to personal suits against the defendant, where the property is not the source of the conflict but is sought as compensation by the plaintiff. The authority of a court exercising quasi in rem jurisdiction is limited to a determination of the respondent's interest in the property."

Federal Jurisdiction

In addition to providing for the creation of the Supreme Court, Article Three of the Constitution also provides for the establishment of Federal courts throughout the country, in every state. Federal courts do not hear all matters that can be brought into a court but rather have specific jurisdictional requirements. The types of cases usually heard in Federal court are admiralty law cases, bankruptcy cases, cases involving ambassadors and ministers, treaty cases and cases involving the constitutionality of a law and disputes between two states.

In some of the above listed cases, it is plainly obvious that these types of cases require Federal court. For example if Maine decided to file a lawsuit against Oregon, in the interest of fairness, the case could not be heard in either state. Also the case could probably not receive an objective hearing in neighboring states, so only Federal courts, which obtain their funding from the Federal government and are not subject to state budgets, can be impartial and unbiased.

One of the Federal court requirements listed in Article Three is that the Court can only exercise judicial powers, or in other words, it can only render decisions for cases that it actually hears. This "case or controversy" requirement means that the Federal courts cannot make social policy or render decisions based upon hypothetical legal questions.

Another requirement for Federal cases has to do with the persons or entities bringing the case before Federal court. Not only must there be an actual case and or controversy, the plaintiff must have actually sustained harm. This requirement is called standing, and the plaintiff must have standing in order to bring the case in Federal court. What this means in practical terms is if your twin sister was cheated out of a lot of money by an unscrupulous mortgage company, you cannot bring the case into Federal court. The only person who can bring the case is your twin sister because she was the person who was actually suffering some type of legal harm, and therefore she is the only one who has standing to bring the case.

The third requirement for Federal cases is that the case must be brought in a Federal court that has the authority to hear the case and to order a remedy. Federal courts are courts of limited jurisdiction and all Federal courts cannot hear all Federal matters, even if the first two requirements have been met. For example, although a person may have a case that meets the case and controversy requirement and he or she may have standing to bring his or her case because he or she actually suffered a legal harm, the person cannot bring his or her Admiralty law case in a Federal Bankruptcy court. The Federal Bankruptcy court does not have the authority to hear Admiralty cases and it cannot provide a remedy for a case of this nature.

One very important requirement for Federal cases is centered around the concept of "mootness". There must be an active or ongoing legal issue that needs to be addressed in order for the Federal Courts to hear the case. The issue must be capable of repetition and must be current. For example, a case brought into Federal Court requesting that the beaches close at five o'clock on every Friday before December 31, 2013,so as not to interfere with the feeding cycle of seals will get tossed out because there is nothing further to be addressed – it is already 2014! The court is unable to provide a remedy for this case and therefore the issue is moot because there is no longer an active or ongoing problem based upon the wording of the complaint.

There are two other very important concepts to remember in relation to Federal courts and what cases they can hear and when. The two requirements involve the jurisdiction of the court. They are federal question jurisdiction and diversity jurisdiction.

Federal question jurisdiction refers to cases that involve disputes between two or more states, cases that involve disputes between the United States and foreign governments, or cases that present questions in relation to the US Constitution, the US Government or Federal laws. For example, if the citizens of the state of Maryland wanted to file suit against the Department of Energy(DOE) for the pollution emitted from a nuclear facility in their state, they would bring the suit against DOE(a US Government Agency) in Federal Court.

State and Federal Court Systems

Most people are somewhat familiar with the Federal court system, but the state court system is often times confusing. As a quick review, it is easy to remember that the highest court in the Federal Court system is the US Supreme Court, which is comprised of one chief justice and eight other justices who are appointed by the President and usually serve until death or retirement.

The next level in the Federal court system is shared by the U.S. Court of Appeals for the 11 numbered circuits, with the DC Circuit on the left hand side of the hierarchy and the US Court of Appeals for the Federal Circuit on the right hand side of the hierarchy. Directly under US Court of Appeals for the 11 circuits and DC Circuit are the US District Court Federal trial courts and the US Tax Court. Directly under the US Court of Appeals for the Federal Circuit are the courts of International Trade (customs and tariff), US Court of Veterans Appeals and the US Court of Claims. The last level for the Federal Court system is the Administrative Agencies on the left hand side of the hierarchy and the US Patent and Trademark Office on the right hand side of the hierarchy.

The US Court of Appeals for the 11 enumerated circuits and the DC circuit is the next level down from the Supreme Court. These courts were called circuit courts because in the past judges had to travel from one place to another to try cases. In essence, they "rode the circuit." The judges in each one of these circuits are responsible for hearing all of the district cases in that region.

The circuits are as follows:

- First Circuit: Maine, Massachusetts, New Hampshire Puerto Rico and Rhode Island
- Second Circuit: Connecticut, New York and Vermont
- Third Circuit: Delaware, New Jersey, Pennsylvania and Virgin Islands
- Fourth Circuit: Maryland, North Carolina, South Carolina, Virginia and West Virginia

- Fifth Circuit: Louisiana, Mississippi, and Texas
- Sixth Circuit: Kentucky, Michigan, Ohio and Tennessee
- Seventh Circuit: Illinois, Indiana, and Wisconsin
- Eighth Circuit: Arkansas, Iowa, Minnesota, Missouri, Nebraska, North Dakota, and South Dakota
- Ninth Circuit: Alaska, California, Guam, Hawaii, Idaho, Montana, Nevada, Northern Mariana Islands, Oregon and Washington
- Tenth Circuit: Colorado, Kansas, New Mexico, Oklahoma, Utah and Wyoming
- Eleventh Circuit: Alabama, Florida and Georgia.

There is the Washington DC Circuit that completes the circuit system.

The United States Court of Appeals for the Federal Circuit has nationwide jurisdiction over some types of appeals. Most administrative agency decisions and rule-making cases are heard by the Court of Appeals for the DC Circuit. Decisions of the Federal courts are published in the Federal Reporters that are published by West. The other Federal Courts primarily hear specialized cases, in that the Tax Court hears tax matters and the Veterans Affairs Courts hear veteran's appeals.

The State Court System is set up in a different manner than the Federal court system. The State Court system usually has more tiers to its hierarchy than the Federal court system. The highest court in the state court system is usually the state supreme court or the court of last resort. Under the State Supreme Court is the next level, which is comprised of the intermediate appellate courts. Only 23 of the 50 states have intermediate appellate courts. Under the appellate courts is the level that contains the Superior Court. The Superior court is the highest trial court with general jurisdiction.

The next level is comprised of the Probate court, the County Courts and the Municipal Courts. The Probate courts hear cases that relate to wills, guardianships/conservatorships, and estate administration. The probate court is called Surrogate's Court or Orphans' Court in some states. The County Courts have limited jurisdiction for civil and criminal cases. These courts are sometimes referred to as Courts of Common Pleas or District Courts. The Municipal Courts hear cases that affect the municipality only. In some jurisdictions the municipal cases are heard by a magistrate or non-lawyer justices. The bottom level of the state court system is the level that contains the Justice of the Peace and the Police Magistrate. These are the lowest courts in the hierarchy and their jurisdiction is very limited.

The other lower level state court is the Domestic Relations Court, which is sometimes called the Family or Juvenile court. This court is very limited in that it only decides family and juvenile matters. There are also specialty courts that may be included in the state court system. Some of the specialty courts include: Small Claims Court, Landlord and Tenant, Youth Court, Drug Court and Consumer Court.

Business Organizations

Perhaps the most common type of business organization in the United States is the sole proprietorship. According to the blog of the federal government's Small Business Association, more than 70 seventy percent of all US businesses are owned and operated as sole proprietorships(17 million).

A sole proprietorship is defined by the Small Business Administration as "an unincorporated business owned and run by one individual (no partners are involved), with no distinction between the business and its owner." The owner of a sole proprietorship is responsible for everything that happens within the business. If the business is successful, he or she does not have to share profits, but if the business fails then he or she suffers the entire loss. Most of all, if the business is sued he or she alone is liable with no means to shield his or her personal assets from a judgment awarded as the result of a lawsuit.

In *Financial Accounting* 14thEdition, Williams, J.(2010)p. 58, the sole proprietor is viewed differently: "From an accounting viewpoint, a sole proprietorship is regarded as a business entity separate from the other financial activities of its owner. From a legal viewpoint, however, the business and its owner are not regarded as separate entities."

There are pros and cons for operating as sole proprietorship and when one takes into account the percentage of businesses in the US that are sole proprietorships, it becomes fairly obvious that most business owners feel that the pros outweigh the cons.

One of the first advantages of a sole proprietorship is the ease with which one can start a business. A sole proprietorship requires few forms and red tape. In most jurisdictions all that is required is a license or permit, payment of a minimal fee and registration with the state ,and a person can operate his or her business as a sole proprietorship. Another advantage is autonomy. A sole proprietor does not have to report to a board of directors; he or she is in charge of the business and he or she does not have to consult with others in order to make decisions. From an accounting perspective, the sole proprietorship is also advantageous because a balance sheet is not needed and reports in triplicate are not necessary. In addition, the money made by the sole proprietorship can be listed on the owner's personal income tax return; there is no need for schedules A-Z and everything in between.

Flexibility is a wonderful and useful feature associated with sole proprietorships. A sole proprietor can usually choose his or her hours and days of work and the business can be closed or terminated without a lot of fanfare. If a sole proprietor does not employ others then he or she need not concern him or herself with unemployment insurance, Medicare, social security, state and federal tax requirements forms that need to be filed monthly, quarterly and annually. Depending on the nature of the work that the sole proprietor performs, he or she can work from his or her home on a full or part-time basis thereby saving the money that office space rental would cost. There are so many advantages to operating as a sole proprietor, it is no wonder there are so many of them in the US. However every venture has a bad side, and if there are advantages then it is a certainty that there are disadvantages as well.

The disadvantages to operating a sole proprietorship are, first and foremost, those of liability. A sole proprietor can lose all of his funds - personal as well as business - as a result of a lawsuit. Since for legal purposes, the business and the owner are considered as one and the same, the sole proprietor's personal assets are available for seizure and are not afforded any type of protection.

Another major disadvantage of sole proprietorships is the difficulty that they face in obtaining funding. Banks and other lending institutions are wary of making loans to persons who are just starting a business. The reluctance increases incrementally if the sole proprietor does not have collateral in the form of inventory or anything that can be liquidated in the event of a default. Some banks will not lend money to a business that is not incorporated, which limits the number of resources a sole proprietor has at his or her disposal.

In addition, unless the sole proprietor has training as an accountant, running a business can be overwhelming at times. Human beings have a difficult time spotting their own errors and in sole proprietorships, there is usually only one set of eyes looking at the financial records. If the sole proprietor does not catch his or her own accounting or arithmetic errors, the results can be disastrous.

General or Limited Partnerships

The next most popular business organization after the sole proprietorship is the partnership. There are two main types of partnerships: General partnerships and limited partnerships.

A general partnership consists of two or more owners of a business who agree to be liable for the debts of the partnership/business. This liability is unlimited and can create huge financial problems for the members of the partnership. For example, Beaver, Cleaver, and Duck are all general partners that own an air limo service, however Duck has a serious drinking and gambling problem. Soon-to-be married couple Lovey and Hank give the general partnership a $10,000 deposit for their honeymoon flight to an undisclosed location. If Duck gets drunk and gambles away the deposit then

Beaver and Cleaver have to refund the deposit to Lovey and Hank. In addition, Beaver and Cleaver as well as Duck are liable for a breach of contract. Beaver and Cleaver have to pay off the debts that Duck incurred because they are all general partners.

In a limited partnership, the partners are only liable to the extent of their contribution. In the above example, if Beaver and Cleaver were limited partners whose initial investment was $1,500 each, then they would have had to only pay 1,500 dollars and the rest would have had to been paid by Duck, the general managing partner. With limited partnerships, there is usually only one general partner. This general partner is in charge and has the most authority in the partnership. The general partner manages the daily operations of the business, has full control of the business and sets the tone for the business. The limited partners do not have a say in the daily operations and do not exercise control or authority within the business.

However, although the limited partners are only liable to the extent of their contribution the general partner assumes most of the responsibility for the bad debts of the business. In the example above, if Duck was the general partner he would have to pay Lovey and Hank $7,000 dollars plus he would be liable for the amount awarded for the breach of contract and any other damages that might have been incurred as a result of his actions. He would not have been able to rely on Beaver and Cleaver to share in the debt equally because they were limited partners with limited liability.

According to QuickMBA.com, the statute that governs limited partnerships is called the Uniform Limited Partnerships Act (ULPA) and dates back to 1916. The act was revised in 1976 and the name was changed to the Revised Uniform Limited Partnership Act (RULPA). The Act was amended in 1985 to address the issue of limited partners who are not members of the board of directors assuming control of the business.

Limited Liability Companies and Joint Ventures

The Small Business Administration defines the Limited liability Company (LLC) as a "hybrid type of legal structure that provides the limited liability features of a corporation and the tax efficiencies and operational flexibility of a partnership whose "owners" are referred to as "members."
The creation of an LLC involves more paperwork and bureaucratic red tape than a partnership or sole proprietorship, but less than for a corporation. In an LLC, the members are not taxed as a separate business entity. Instead, all profits and losses are "passed through" the business to each member of the LLC.

Although each state has separate requirements for the creation of an LLC, there are several general principles that govern the formation of an LLC. They are:

1. The LLC must pick a business name that is not already in use within that state. The name selected must include the words Limited Company or LLC.

2. The company must file a document known as the articles of organization. The articles of organization list the names and contact information of the members of the LLC. Most articles of organization are filed with the Secretary of the State's office.

3. The company should create an operating agreement. "The operating agreement usually includes percentage of interests, allocation of profits and losses, member's rights and responsibilities and other provisions."

4. After the LLC is registered with the Secretary of State, all business licenses, permits and so forth must be obtained.

5. Finally, some states require that an LLC post a notice in the newspaper announcing and informing the general public that it is now doing business as a Limited Liability Company (LLC).

A joint venture is defined by Investopedia as "A business arrangement in which two or more parties agree to pool their resources for the purpose of accomplishing a specific task. This task can be a new project or any other business activity. In a joint venture (JV), each of the participants is responsible for profits, losses and costs associated with it. However, the venture is its own entity, separate and apart from the participants' other business interests."

A joint venture allows persons to engage in a single profitmaking business opportunity without becoming a part of a corporation or without becoming a member of a partnership. Most joint venture do not last more than four years.

One of the chief complaints about joint ventures is that they restrict competition and can create quasi-monopolistic situations if the persons who make up the joint venture were previously competitors. For example, if there are three taxi companies in a small city and if all three taxi companies form a joint venture in order to fund an airport limo service, the citizens of the city will suffer because there will be little, if any, competition among the taxi companies. Whereas before one taxi company charged 5 dollars for a one mile ride, another $4.50 for the ride and the third taxi company charged 6.00 dollars for the same one mile ride, the taxi passengers would be greatly affected if the three taxi companies formed the joint venture and set the cab fare at 6 dollars or even 5 dollars. Since the three taxi companies are now part of the joint venture, there is no real need for them to compete so now they will cooperate with each other to the detriment of the passengers.

It should be noted that Congress has revised and amended legislation in the last thirty years to reflect the growing popularity of the joint ventures. In 1982 Congress amended the Sherman Anti-Trust Act of 1890 (15 U.S.C.A. § 6a)—the statutory basis of antitrust law—to ease restrictions on joint ventures that involve exports. At the same time, it passed the Export Trading Company Act (U.S.C.A. § 4013) to grant exporters limited immunity to antitrust prosecution. Two years later, the National Cooperative Research Act of 1984 (Pub. L. No. 98-462) permitted ventures involved in joint research and development to notify the government of their joint venture and thus limit their liability in the event of prosecution for antitrust violations. This protection against liability was expanded in 1993 to include some joint ventures involving production (Pub. L. No. 103-42).

Finally, a joint venture can be terminated by the death of any of the members, when the desired funding is obtained, when the date that was previously agreed upon is reached and when there is some much turmoil that a judicial officer must terminate the joint venture, because its continuation is neither effective nor practical.

Corporations

Although sole proprietorships are the most common type of business organization in the United States, corporations are probably the most recognized type of business organization. The average US citizen is inundated with corporate brand information from the time he or she rises in the morning. Whereas he or she may not encounter a sole proprietorship until he or she leaves home, the morning starts with products produced by corporate giants: Proctor and Gamble make shampoos and soaps, and some part of the breakfast meal is usually provided by either the Kellogg's, General Mills and/or Coca Cola corporate entities.

What constitutes a corporation? A corporation is defined by Merriam-Webster as:
"A body formed and authorized by law to act as a single person although constituted by one or more persons and legally endowed with various rights and duties including the capacity of succession."

A corporation is an artificial entity created to act as a human person would. However, a corporation is made up of several people that act as one person.

A corporation has to register a charter with the state, and articles of incorporation have to be filed with the Secretary of the State. Before the incorporation process is explained, it would be helpful to note that the most important reasons for forming a corporation are:

1. A corporation provides for limited liability for its owners because it has separate legal standing from its owners
2. A corporation can issue shares that can be transferred with little difficulty
3. The death or retirement of its owners does not terminate or dissolve the corporation
4. There are distinct tax advantages to incorporation.
5. It is easier to obtain financing for an incorporated business because a majority of banks and lenders will not make loans to businesses that are not incorporated.

The steps needed to form a corporation as reported on the Small Business Information website are as follows:

1. Choose a Corporate Name & Address: Have a corporate name search performed to ensure you are unique and have no trade mark problems in the future.
2. Select a State to Incorporate: Setting up a corporation will be easier and cheaper in your home state.
3. Select a Corporation Type: Determine the best type of corporation for your business--LLC, S corporation or C Corporation.
4. Determine Company Directors: Directors of the company and positions will have to be filed within the Articles of Incorporation and By-laws.
5. Choose Your Share Type: Corporations can issue common and preferred stock. Select the best for your situation.
6. Obtain Certificate of Incorporation: Available from local State office or business retailer.

7. Process & File Incorporation: Your incorporation can be completed by a lawyer or a do-it-yourself kit. Finally, file your incorporation with a Registered Agent.

The Articles of Incorporation and the Bylaws are the backbone of the corporation. These two documents explain in detail how the corporation will operate, and under what governance. The Articles of Incorporation are sometimes called the charter and contain general information regarding the legal name, location, contact information and purpose of the corporation. The Articles of Incorporation must be filed in order to establish the corporation within the state. Contained in the Articles should be the name and contact information for the registered agent, person who is authorized to receive legal documents and service of process on behalf of the corporation. The Articles of Incorporation list the number of shares the company is authorized to issue and the minimum value per share.

According to Litigation Essentials (hosted at Lexis Nexis,) "most states amended their "charter option' statutes that authorize corporations to include provisions in their charters eliminating the personal liability of directors for money damages for breach of certain duties, such as breach of a duty of care. Following the Delaware Supreme Court's ruling in Smith v. Van Gorkom that the business judgment rule does not protect corporate directors from liability for gross negligence, almost all states have amended their corporate statutes in order to reduce the liability exposure of, and increase financial protection for, directors and sometimes, officers. This chapter discusses the impact of state exculpatory legislation on director liability."

The Bylaws are documents that explain the operation of the corporation. The Bylaws explain the duties of the directors and officers, as well as list the rules by which the corporation will be governed. Bylaws are internal documents. The Bylaws do not have to be filed with the Secretary of State as the Articles of Incorporation do. However, corporations are required to keep the Bylaws at their primary business location. Even though the Bylaws do not address or mention the amount of stock that can be issued, they establish the voting rights of the company's shareholders based on their class of stock ownership, because shareholders who own preferred stock have voting privileges that are different from those of common shareholders.

One major difference between Articles of Incorporation and Bylaws involves the amendment of the documents. In order to amend the Articles of Incorporation to reflect a change in address, registered agent, etc., an amendment must be filed with the Secretary of State and the applicable fee must be paid. If the Bylaws need to be amended, a vote of the directors and shareholders must be held before the rules are changed or amended and a majority of the company's shareholders must agree to change or amend the bylaws. Since the Bylaws are internal documents not filed with the State, no fee is required to amend or change the Bylaws.

Types of Corporations and Corporate Taxation

One important consideration for incorporation is the selection of corporation types, especially the tax consequences related to the types. There are three types of corporations: the C-corporation, the S-corporation and the LLC.

All corporations start out as C-corporations. The Internal Revenue Service explains the tax consequences of a c-corporation as follows:

"For federal income tax purposes, a C corporation is recognized as a separate taxpaying entity. A corporation conducts business, realizes net income or loss, pays taxes and distributes profits to shareholders. The profit of a corporation is taxed to the corporation when earned, and then is taxed to the shareholders when distributed as dividends. This creates a double tax. The corporation does not get a tax deduction when it distributes dividends to shareholders. Shareholders cannot deduct any loss of the corporation."

The basic C-corporation is taxed twice, but that is not the case with the S-corporation. An S-corporation gets its name from Subchapter S of the Internal Revenue Code. In order to be considered an S-corp, Form 2553 must be filed with the IRS and all S corporation guidelines must be fulfilled so that the corporation can obtain special tax status. This special tax status allows the S-corp to be considered a pass-through entity. This means that S-corps must file Form 1120S with the Internal Revenue Service, however, no income tax is paid at the corporate level which means there is no double taxation. The business' profits and or losses are then passed through the business. The profits and losses are then reported on the owners' personal tax returns. Taxes that are owed are paid by the owners, not the business.

Corporate ownership is restricted to 100 shareholders for S- corporations, but there are no restrictions for C-corp. owners. S-corps can have only one class of stock but C-corporations can and do have various classes of stock.

An LLC is not a corporation but it can be taxed as a corporation. An LLC, which stands for Limited Liability Company, is a hybrid of a partnership and a corporation. It performs daily management activities like a partnership but has limited liability like a corporation. LLCs do not have partners or shareholders, the owners are called members. Whereas the LLC is not recognized by the Internal Revenue Service as a separate taxing entity, the LLC can elect to be taxed as a corporation.

Since the LLC is a hybrid of a partnership and a corporation it enjoys the better tax advantages found in partnerships along with the flexibility of a partnership and limited personal liability inherent in corporations.

Types of Stocks

There are several types and classes of stocks. The two main or most commonly known types of stock are common and preferred stocks.

- Common stocks are the basic form of capital stock. Persons who purchase common stocks acquire the usual and traditional rights associated with stock ownership: voting rights, dividends, and claim to the residual assets if there is liquidation. The majority of stocks issued are Common stocks and common stocks produce the highest returns of any investment in the long term.

- Preferred stocks are distinguished from common stocks because they have preference over common stocks in terms of dividends. They also have cumulative dividend rights but they do not confer voting power. One important characteristic of preferred stock is that the holders are paid off before the common stock owners in the event of liquidation of the company.

Other types of stock include the following:

- Blue Chip stocks: these are stocks from old line profitable companies. These stocks reflect a sometimes century old record of high and stable earnings. They almost always pay dividends.

- Growth stocks are ones that do not pay dividends because the earnings are reinvested to continue growth. Although they are usually expected to have high earnings and can provide great increases when there is a problem the price of the shares can drop greatly. There is a lot of fluctuation in these stocks.

- Penny Stocks can be purchased for as low as a few dollars per share and these stocks are not usually traded on the major exchanges. Even though the initial investment is small, these stocks represent a great risk. Penny stocks are an example of speculative stocks.

- Treasury Stock, as defined by Investorwords.com, is "[stock that] is issued but not outstanding and is not taken into consideration when calculating earnings per share or dividends or for voting purposes."

- Value Stocks are stocks that investors think are being traded lower than their market value and many investors believe that this type of stock can provide long-term growth because the stocks are perceived as undervalued.
- Watered-down stock is a type of stock that has a value that is worth less than the amount invested in it. This "watering down" causes problems in terms of low market value, little or no return on investment and liquidity options.

In addition to types of stocks there are other terms relating to stocks that paralegals should know. Some of the terms are:

- Stock split, which occurs when the number of shares of stock is increased but the value of the shares is decreased

- Stock options, which are contracts or agreements that authorize or allow the stockholder to buy or sell shares of stock at a specific price for a specified time frame without having to adhere to what the market price is for that time. There are call and put options which are also stock options and can be purchased in advance if the investor wants to speculate or "hedge"

- Stock redemption rules and rights, which are a way of "cashing out" or buying out some of the shareholders. When there are less shareholders, the remaining shareholders have more control and a larger part in the company.

- Stock or preemptive rights refer to the chosen shareholders who can maintain an unchanging percentage of the company's stock. These special stockholders are given first preference to purchase new stock in keeping with what they already own. For example if Stockie B owns 20% of the old shares, he or she is given first crack at 20% of the new offerings.

- A stock subscription is a legal contract whereby a purchaser is given latitude to purchase a certain amount of shares at a specific price at a specific later date. Down payments are often required and the subscription is often paid in installments.

- Stock warrants are very similar to stock subscriptions because they give the holder the right to purchase shares of stock for specific price and at a specific time. Warrants however, are issued and guaranteed by the company and the lifetime of warrants is measured in years not months.

- Short term share trading is very risky and can be nerve-wracking. Day trading is a form of short term share trading; these trades can and do last from a few days to a few weeks. Investors have to watch carefully to see how the stock is trending in the short run and then make their decision to buy or sell.

Securities and Regulations

The term "Securities" is used to refer to shares of stock, bonds, and debentures issued by corporations and governments. The term "Securities" is used because the assets and/or the profits of the corporation or the credit of the government are used as the security for payment. Most securities are highly regulated and most are traded on stock and bond markets. Some of the more commonly known stock markets are the New York Stock Exchange, American Stock Exchange, and NASDQ.

Although Equity and Debt securities are both used to help companies finance their operations, Debt securities are by far the safer of the two securities. Debt securities, also known as fixed income securities, are defined by Investopedia as:

"Any debt instrument that can be bought or sold between two parties and has basic terms defined, such as notional amount (amount borrowed), interest rate and maturity/renewal date. Debt securities include government bonds, corporate bonds, CDs, municipal bonds, preferred stock, collateralized securities (such as CDOs, CMOs, GNMAs) and zero-coupon securities."

Equity Securities as defined by the Legal Information Institute as:

"...include(ing) any stock or similar security, certificate of interest or participation in any profit sharing agreement, preorganization certificate or subscription, transferable share, voting trust certificate or certificate of deposit for an equity security, limited partnership interest, interest in a joint venture, or certificate of interest in a business trust; any security future on any such security; or any security convertible, with or without consideration into such a security, or carrying any warrant or right to subscribe to or purchase such a security; or any such warrant or right; or any put, call, straddle, or other option or privilege of buying such a security from or selling such a security to another without being bound to do so."

Equity securities have the right to share in dividends, the right to vote, and the right to a proportionate share of net assets upon liquidation of the corporation. The owners of equity securities, who are called shareholders or stockholders, are able to profit from capital gains, but holders of debt securities can only receive interest and the repayment of the principal.

Securities are regulated by the Securities and Exchange Commission (SEC) and all states have Blue sky Laws that are designed to protect investors from fraudulent sales of securities. These Blue Sky laws as stated by the SEC "require companies making small offerings to register their offerings before they can be sold in a particular state." The first Blue Sky Law was enacted in Kansas in 1911. There are a number of Federal laws that govern or affect securities sales and trading. Definitions and explanations for these laws have been provided at the SEC website and are listed below:

- The Securities Act of 1933 – often referred to as the "truth in securities" law, the Securities Act of 1933 has two basic objectives: Require that investors receive financial and other significant information concerning securities being offered for public sale; and prohibit deceit, misrepresentations and other fraud in the sale of securities.

- The Securities Exchange Act of 1934 - Created the Securities and Exchange Commission. The Act empowers the SEC with broad authority over all aspects of the securities industry. This includes the power to register, regulate, and oversee brokerage firms, transfer agents, and clearing agencies as well as the nation's securities self regulatory organizations (SROs). The various securities exchanges, such as the New York Stock Exchange, the NASDAQ Stock Market, and the Chicago Board of Options are SROs. The Financial Industry Regulatory Authority (FINRA) is also an SRO.

- Trust Indenture Act of 1939 - This Act applies to debt securities such as bonds, debentures, and notes that are offered for public sale. Even though such securities may be registered under the Securities Act, they may not be offered for sale to the public unless a formal agreement between the issuer of bonds and the bondholder, known as the trust indenture, conforms to the standards of this Act.

- Investment Company Act of 1940 - This Act regulates the organization of companies, including mutual funds, that engage primarily in investing, reinvesting, and trading in securities, and whose own securities are offered to the investing public. The regulation is designed to minimize conflicts of interest that arise in these complex operations. The Act requires these companies to disclose their financial condition and investment policies to investors when stock is initially sold and, subsequently, on a regular basis. The focus of this Act is on disclosure to the investing public of information about the fund and its investment objectives, as well as on investment company structure and operations. It is important to remember that the Act does not permit the SEC to directly supervise the investment decisions or activities of these companies or judge the merits of their investments.

- Investment Advisers Act of 1940 - This law regulates investment advisers. With certain exceptions, this Act requires that firms or sole practitioners compensated for advising others about securities investments must register with the SEC and conform to regulations designed to protect investors. Since the Act was amended in 1996 and 2010, generally only advisers who have at least $100 million of assets under management or advise a registered investment company must register with the Commission.

- Sarbanes-Oxley Act of 2002 - On July 30, 2002, President George W. Bush signed into law the Sarbanes-Oxley Act of 2002, which he characterized as "the most far reaching reforms of American business practices since the time of Franklin Delano Roosevelt." The Act mandated a number of reforms to enhance corporate responsibility, enhance financial disclosures and combat corporate and accounting fraud, and created the "Public Company Accounting Oversight Board," also known as the PCAOB, to oversee the activities of the auditing profession.

- Dodd-Frank Wall Street Reform and Consumer Protection Act of 2010 - The Dodd-Frank Wall Street Reform and Consumer Protection Act were signed into law on July 21, 2010 by President Barack Obama. The legislation set out to reshape the U.S. regulatory system in a number of areas including but not limited to consumer protection, trading restrictions, credit ratings, regulation of financial products, corporate governance and disclosure, and transparency.

- Jumpstart Our Business Startups Act of 2012 - The Jumpstart Our Business Startups Act (the "JOBS Act") was enacted on April 5, 2012. The JOBS Act aims to help businesses raise funds in public capital markets by minimizing regulatory requirements.

Even with all of the regulations and laws in place to prevent securities fraud there still news headlines that bespeak of the latest securities infractions. No matter how many laws are passed there will always be some unscrupulous companies that will find ways to circumvent the laws. To that end, it is a reasonable certainty that more securities laws will be added to the list that is in place today.

Corporate Dissolution and Piercing the Corporate Veil

There is more than one way in which a corporation can be dissolved. One of the ways involve voluntary dissolution and one involves an involuntary dissolution. All states have laws that provide for the dissolution of corporations.

There are specific steps that must be taken to dissolve a corporation. Before you fill out a single form, the board of directors should hold a meeting to make certain that dissolution of the corporation is what is warranted and desired at that time. Even if the board of directors agree that dissolution is necessary, the real test will be the vote of the shareholders. In order to close a corporation, a majority of the shareholders must agree to the dissolution.

There will be tax consequences as a result of the dissolution. Therefore, the Internal Revenue Service must be notified of the impending dissolution. Unless there is a specific exception most corporations have 30 days to file form 966 with the IRS.

All licenses, permits and legal names must be cancelled and the corporation's creditors and debtors must be notified. After the notice process is over, the debts and taxes need to be paid. Once these items are paid then the assets based on the number of shares must be given out to the shareholders. Finally the Articles of Dissolution have to be filed to let your state, customers and the general public know that your corporation no longer exists.

Another way that corporations ultimately end up dissolved is the doctrine that allows for piercing veil. What this term means is that the court will allow the corporate owners' limited liability protection to be lifted or set aside. One of the main benefits of a corporation is that it provides for limited liability. When that benefit is taken away, the corporation often times dissolves or dies out because there virtually are no assets to be had, personal or otherwise.

The courts do not readily allow for the piercing of the corporate veil. Usually, it is only allowed in very serious cases. Some of the reasons for piercing the corporate veil include undercapitalization of the entity before incorporation, misrepresentation and fraudulent business practices.

Corporate Terms to Know

- Closely held corporation – according to BizTaxLaw.com, this "is a corporation in which more than half of the shares are held by fewer than five individuals. Closely held corporations are private companies, and are not publicly held. In a closely held corporation, if one of the shareholders wants to sell some or all of his/her shares, the sale must take place with one of the other existing shareholders, since no sale of shares can take place."

- Publicly held corporation – BizTaxLaw.com defines this as "a stock corporation in which the shares of stock are available to the public. The shares are traded on the open market through a stock exchange."

- Mergers & Acquisitions (M&A) – according to InvestingAnswers.com, this term "refers to the management, financing, and strategy involved with buying, selling, and combining companies... A merger is the combination of two similarly sized companies combined to form a new company. An acquisition occurs when one company clearly purchases another and becomes the new owner. A merger or an acquisition usually starts out with a series of informal discussions between the boards of the companies, followed by formal negotiation, a letter of intent, due diligence, a purchase or merger agreement, and finally, the execution of the deal and the transfer of payment."

- Corporation by Estoppel – USLegal.com defines the term in this way: "Corporation by estoppel refers to one who contracts and deals with an entity as a corporation thereby admits that the entity is a corporation and is estopped to deny its incorporation in an action arising out of the contract or course of dealing. Corporation by estoppel is a concept conceived and applied in equity to avoid injustice and unfairness."

- De Jure Corporation – Investopedia says, "A business that has fulfilled its requirements for formation according to the regulations for earning a state charter. De jure, meaning "a matter of law," indicates that the company has been fully and legally chartered, and is therefore entitled to do business. A de jure corporation is one that is lawfully chartered by a state government, and is recognized as a corporation for all purposes."

- De Facto Corporation – USLegal.com says a de facto corporation "is one that has acted in good faith and would be an ordinary corporation but for failure to comply with some technical requirements."

- Convertible shares/securities – the SEC says "A 'convertible security' is a security—usually a bond or a preferred stock—that can be converted into a different security—typically shares of the company's common stock. In most cases, the holder of the convertible determines whether and when to convert. In other cases, the company has the right to determine when the conversion occurs."

Civil Litigation

Civil litigation is the name given to legal causes of actions that are governed by either the Federal or State Rules of Civil Procedure. Civil litigation differs from criminal litigation in that remedies are different as well as the burdens of proof. Criminal cases are governed by the Rules of Criminal Procedure not civil Procedure.

The first concept that should be addressed is the difference in remedies. It is helpful to refresh our memories as to what a remedy is in legal terms. A remedy is a means or way for the court to administer justice by awarding a judgment, issuing and injunction or dispensing a penalty. In criminal litigation, the desired outcome is criminal punishment of the person who has committed a crime.

It should be noted that in civil litigation, the parties are usually private individuals, corporations or other entities. The captions for civil cases are as follows: Bullock versus Tyler. In criminal cases, the parties are the state, county or municipality versus the person that is accused of committing a criminal act. The caption for criminal cases is then State of Texas versus Thomas Reed.

There are other differences that are noticeable as well. Civil litigation has a lesser burden of proof than criminal cases. The burden of proof for civil litigation is "The preponderance of the evidence" which contrasts with the burden of proof in criminal litigation which is "beyond a reasonable doubt." This makes it very clear that the stakes are much higher in criminal court.

Civil court is designed to address torts and other nonviolent actions that persons or companies inflict on one another. Criminal court, on the other hand, is designed to deal with persons and sometimes companies who have caused serious injury or death to members of society. The stakes are much higher because in civil court, a defendant may lose the shirt off his back but he will not lose his life. That is not the case in civil litigation.

A civil litigation or lawsuit is commenced by filing a summons and complaint with the court. The first thing that a person needs to know is in which court he or she should file their complaint. Now even if a paralegal knows that the complaint is not a criminal case, she still has to figure out which of the civil courts would be the appropriate court in which to file. Most towns have several civil courts: Circuit court, Federal court, District court Small claims court, Family court, landlord and tenant court, Probate court, Traffic court, Bankruptcy court and Municipal court. So how does one decide in which court to file?

The first thing is to determine what the case is about and then to determine which court has jurisdiction. Assuming that a person knows what the issues are in the case that he or she is trying to file, the question becomes which court is qualified to hear that type of case. Just as a person would not go to a foot doctor for treatment of a migraine headache, a person would not usually file a slip and fall case in probate or traffic court.

So how does one find jurisdiction? Jurisdiction is defined as the authority or power that a court has to hear a specific type of case. Sometimes there is more than one court that has the authority to hear the specific type of case. In cases like this, we refer to the other court or courts as having **concurrent jurisdiction.** If a paralegal still does not know if the court has jurisdiction over the matter that he or she needs to file, she can either visit the court website, consult the rules of the courts, ask a more experienced paralegal or call the court clerk and ask.

Now that the jurisdiction has been decided, what about the venue? Some folks start with venue questions first but unless the civil action occurred in another area, most of the time the venue will be in the area where you are located since you are initiating the action. Venue rules were created so that cases could be heard in the area in which the action occurred or at least in an area that is convenient to the parties. What this means is that if all of the actions occurred in Sweetwater, Mississippi you cannot file the civil suit in Honolulu because you would like to visit Hawaii.

So far so good, you have your venue, you have your court of jurisdiction figured out and hopefully you know who you are suing. Now what? You need to put your information in an orderly fashion and give it to the court. Courts have rules as to how you can present cases to them for review. A good paralegal can look on the court website for sample forms and the rules required for filing a civil lawsuit. Some states, most notably California, will not accept documents that are line numbered in the margins. The best legal minds in the world could have drafted the case, but if there are no line numbers in the margins, the clerk will reject the filing. The best way to avoid this type of problem is to research the filing requirements.

While the paralegal is researching the document requirements she needs to find out how much it will cost to file the summons and complaint. There is a cost to file the documents unless a person is approved to proceed *In Forma Pauperis* (IFP). Proceeding IFP means that a person does not have adequate funds to pay filing fees. There are instances in which a party automatically qualifies to proceed IFP in civil matters. Some of the qualifications that automatically grant IFP status are if the filer is a recipient of food stamps, SNAP, WIC, Section 8 or any other state or Federal subsidy programs. If he or she is indigent but is not receiving benefits then his or her application is reviewed by the judge and it is up to his or her discretion whether to grant IFP status.

Before the paralegal files the summons and complaint, she needs to make sure that she has the correct name and contact information for all parties. The summons, which is defined as a notice from the court to appear in court and defend the lawsuit, will be served to the defendant at his or her last known address. Therefore, it is very important that the contact info is accurate.

The complaint is just that; it is the legal document in which you get the chance to tell the defendant and the court what the other party did wrong and ask the court to punish them by making them either pay or refrain from doing something. While the complaint is being filed, in it is essential that a person remember the one adage from the Bible "Where there is no law, there is no transgression." What that means is even if the person is the worst thing since Lucifer himself, you as the person bringing the suit must include the specific law that he or she violated in the lawsuit.

Once the summons and complaint have been filed, the other party has from 20 to 30 days to file an answer. There are case management conferences, pre-trial hearings, status conferences and discovery schedules involved in civil litigation. Some civil litigations are simple. The plaintiff files the summons and complaint but the defendant does not reply in a timely fashion. The plaintiff asks for a default judgment, the court grants the default judgment against the defendant for disobeying the court and before you know it, the case is over. Civil cases like the one just described rarely happen; the more likely scenario is that the case will drag on for so long that the parties begin to forget salient facts. Since civil litigation is not subject to the speedy trial rules that govern criminal cases, there are lots of rules that help preserve testimony and evidence in the event that the parties die or grow senile before the case ends.

One of the first events geared towards preserving evidence and possibly avoiding a lengthy trial is the case management conference, or the pretrial meeting. In these meet and greet sessions the parties have the opportunity to size each other up and decide if they think they should proceed with the litigation. Sometimes after these meetings, the parties reach a settlement or an agreement between them that will prevent a lengthy trial.

If a settlement cannot be reached, the opposing party will usually file a motion based upon Federal Rule 12 (b) (6) or a similar state rule. The 12(b) (6) motion to dismiss simply states that the plaintiff has failed to state a claim upon which relief may be granted. What this actually means is that the opposing party is saying that you have a weak case that you cannot win based upon the facts you have alleged. At this point the plaintiff must immediately counter this motion or else it will be granted. This process can go on for some time.

The next step in civil litigation is the discovery phase. In the discovery phase, the parties have the opportunity to show each other the evidence, witnesses and documents they plan to use at trial. Discovery is comprised of request for production of documents in which a request is made for all documents that are not attorney client privileged and may be germane to the issues of the case be either copied or made available for inspection for the opposing counsel. The other discovery tools are interrogatories, which are a set of questions sent from one party to the opposing side asking for specific information that relates to the case. The next discovery tool is the Request for Admissions, a set of statements that are usually not true that the opposing side thinks that you will be crazy enough to admit or agree to what they have written.

The most expensive – and probably the most effective – discovery practice is the deposition. The deposition is a meeting in which a person is asked questions under oath. A transcript is made of everything said at the deposition. It is like a mini trial in more ways than one. Many people have found themselves in hot water, because they have been impeached by their deposition statements. What that means is if the witness said the car was a green Ford in a deposition a year ago but he now says that it was blue Chevy, heads will roll. Now it could be a case of memory lapse but opposing counsel will use the deposition testimony to impeach the witness. The witness will come across looking like a big liar even if he or she is not, and his or her credibility is totally shot.

One last word on depositions to remember before we move on to the trial phase: Depositions and affidavits are great to have when the case has been going on for a long time because in the event that a witness is no longer available to testify, there is still a sworn statement detailing the events upon which the case is based.

Civil Litigation Terms

Now that we have introduced a few procedural steps used in civil litigation, the next step is the introduction of more legal terms specific to civil litigation. Not only does a paralegal need to know where a legal document should be filed and which court has jurisdiction, he or she needs to know the names and definitions of the legal documents in mind.

This next section will provide a brief list of legal terms and pleadings along with their definitions and examples of when the documents are utilized. The list begins as follows:

- Affidavit: a sworn statement that is notarized. Affidavits are great tools to have when there is a high probability that the affiant may not be available for trial i.e. in cases in which an affiant is gravely ill or lives in another country.

- Affirmative defenses: statements or justifications given by the defendant that will nullify the plaintiff's cause of actions. For example the plaintiff has established and provided evidence of negligence in his or her complaint. All of the elements of negligence have been met, however the defendant can raise the affirmative defense of laches which states that the plaintiff "sat on her rights" because her or she did not file his or her complaint in a timely fashion.

- Binding: this term essentially means that the decision made is final and cannot be appealed to another court or subject to concurrent jurisdiction.

- Citation: this term refers to the name, case number, volume and page number upon which a particular case is found. For example the citation: Wilson v. Ford, 981 F3d 77 indicates that Wilson case can be found on page 77 of volume 981 of the Federal Reporter third edition. There is a Uniform Book of Citations commonly referred to as the "Blue Book" that lists the correct format for writing citations.

- Counterclaim: the term given for a cause of action brought by a defendant; submitted with the defendant's answer to the plaintiff's complaint.

- Default judgment: this refers to a decision made by the court when a defendant does not answer to plaintiff's complaint within the allotted time frame. Some types of cases cannot be resolved by default judgments, i.e. divorce cases involving children and/or property. Also default judgments can be set aside if the defendant can provide a valid reason for the default i.e. defendant was in the intensive care unit during the time immediately before and during the default deadline.

- Demurrer: this term used to indicate the challenge to the plaintiff's allegations. In a demurrer, the defendant admits that the facts stated in the plaintiff's case are true but the facts are not strong or compelling enough for the plaintiff to win his case.

- Ex parte: this is a term that refers to one party having communication with the judge without the presence or input from the other party. In some cases, an ex parte hearing is necessary to prevent additional harm. Most domestic violence restraining orders are granted ex parte.

- Forum non convenience: this refers to the grounds for dismissal of a cause of action because the location in which the matter was filed would be inconvenient for the defendant. For example: Plaintiff files a lawsuit in Alaska based upon actions that occurred in Alabama; defendant lives in Alabama and has no substantial ties with Alaska. The case will more than likely be dismissed for forum non convenience, because it is unfair and inconvenient to demand that a defendant travel across the country for a case.

- Hearsay Evidence: Statements made by anyone outside of court and not under oath that are offered to prove the truth of an allegation. Unless these statements fall under one of the hearsay exceptions, the statements will not be allowed in court. Some of the hearsay exceptions include: dying declarations, excited utterance, present sense impression and present physical condition.

- Hostile witness: this refers to a person who will not present testimony that will benefit your case. A hostile witness does not have to be overtly antagonistic or hostile, the term simply means that he or she can and will present testimony that is adverse to your litigation.

- In Limine: this term usually refers to a request or motion made before the trial has begun. One of the more common in limine motions is a request to exclude certain statements or other evidence.

- Long arm statute: laws that allow causes of actions to be brought against nonresidents in some instances. Child support enforcement cases regularly use long arm statutes to bring suit against a delinquent, non-custodial parent who resides in another state.

- Motion for trial de novo: this is a request to have a new trial because the judge made an error or failed to correct an error made during the previous trial.

- Replevin: this is a common law remedy that requires that property that was illegally or wrongly taken from a party be returned to the rightful owner. This term is rarely used in most states today, however.

- Sua Sponte: this Latin term refers to decisions made by the judge without motion or requests from either party. In essence these types of decisions are made by the judge voluntarily based on his own discretion.

- Subpoena Duces Tecum: **a** Latin term that refers to an order sent by the court requiring a witness to appear and bring documents specified within the subpoena.

- Voir Dire: this refers to the jury selection process. During *voir dire*, counsel for both sides question potential jurors in order to determine bias based upon previous knowledge, vocation and prejudice.

There are hundreds of terms that a paralegal will encounter in civil litigation. Some of them are obscure and rarely used. However, frequent use of other terms have made it necessary to to abbreviate and/or use acronyms in courts and law firms. A couple of the abbreviated forms include: IFP for *in forma pauperis*, TRO for temporary restraining order and QUADRO for qualified domestic relations order.

Contracts

Contract law is the one area of law that will affect just about every sane, mentally competent US resident over 18 years of age. Some people may never set foot in a court or be involved in a lawsuit, but just about everyone enters into a contract at some point in their life.

The Merriam Webster dictionary defines a contract as "a binding agreement between two or more persons or parties." Black's Online Law Dictionary explains that a contract is "A deliberate engagement between competent parties, upon a legal consideration, to do, or abstain from doing, some act."

Unilateral Contract

People enter contracts every minute of the day. Some of these contracts are unilateral and some are bilateral. The major difference is that a unilateral contract is formed when only one party promises to pay or makes an offer to another party in exchange for performance of some act. An example of the unilateral contract is an insurance policy. The person with the policy pays the insurance company and the insurance company promises to provide health coverage if the party falls ill.

Bilateral Contract

A bilateral contract is an agreement between two or more persons or parties in which both parties make an agreement or promise to each other. They both promise to be bound by the contract. An example of a bilateral contract is: Jared signs a contract to sell Ed a restored 1957 convertible for $35,000 dollars. When Ed gives Jared the money, Jared must give Ed the car and the title.

Implied Contract

An implied contract is an agreement created by the parties' actions, as opposed to their express words. The parties' actions give notice to their assumed intentions. The terms of the contract are understood, but are not usually written or even spoken. For example when a person boards a public transit bus it is understood that unless told otherwise he is agreeing to pay the posted fare.

Express Contract

An express contract is an agreement in which the terms of the agreement are stated with specificity, verbally or written. An example of an express contract is a lease between a landlord and tenant.

Quasi Contract

A quasi contract is an agreement that is not really a contract, but functions like one. This is a legal invention created by the courts as a legal remedy in situations in which unjust enrichment would result if a quasi-contract or implied-in-law contract was not implemented. For example, a family knowingly accepts groceries each week from a grocery delivery service even though they knew that the groceries were meant for their neighbors. A quasi-contract would be created so that the family could not be unjustly enriched by the free food without paying.

Void Contract

A void contract is one that is invalid from the start because the parties or items contracted for are all illegal or wrong. For example, a contract to provide services to illegal aliens crossing the American border. The parties are contracting to engage in illegal acts, and performance is not going to be enforceable because it would require the party or parties to perform illegal acts. No court would uphold or entertain such a "contract."

Voidable Contract

A voidable contract is a contract that has been declared invalid by one or more parties for legal reasons. An example of a voidable contract would one in which one of the parties was mentally unstable but the other party was not aware of the party's mental infirmity at the beginning of the contract.

Unenforceable Contract

Unenforceable contracts are ones in which the contract can be set aside due to undue influence, duress, mistake, misrepresentation, nondisclosure, unconscionability, or impossibility. Contracts can be declared unenforceable if they violate public policy or due to the lack of capacity of one or more parties to the contract. An example of a contract that would be unenforceable due to non-disclosure is: A contracts to sell B his car for 25,000 dollars. He tells B that the car is in pristine condition and has never had problems of any sort. B finds out that he car was under water for 2 weeks as a result of a flood. B states that since A did not disclose the fact that the car was underwater for 2 weeks the contract is unenforceable due to non-disclosure.

Executory Contract

Another distinction to be made in contract is whether the contract is executory or executed. An executory contract is one in which the contract or required action has not been fully performed or completed. An example of an executory contract is: C made a wedding dress for B but has yet to pick up the dress or pay C.

Executed Contract

An executed contract is one in which the required actions of one or all parties have been completed. An example of an executed contract is: Z made a birthday cake for Q's daughter's party; Q paid Z and took delivery of the birthday cake. The contract is executed because the paries have fulfilled their respective obligations or tasks.

Mutual Assent

Mutual assent is one of the required elements of a contract. Clearpoint.law.com defines mutual assent as:

"The two-way agreement between parties with the intent to form a contract. Mutual assent takes the form of offer and acceptance, referred to as a meeting of the minds. It signifies the moment at which an agreement is reached, assuming all other legal requirements are in place."

If the parties cannot agree on the terms of a contract then they do not have a meeting of the minds - mutual assent - and certainly do not have an agreement if they cannot agree on the terms.

An example of a would-be contract that fails due to lack of mutual assent is as follows: Carrie asks Paul to make her Wedgewood Blue brocade seat covers for dining chairs; they both agree the price for the covers should be 125 dollars per chair and there are eight dining room chairs. They both agree that the chairs should be completed and ready for delivery on the Wednesday before Easter. However, Paul does not carry Wedgewood blue brocade cloth, he only carries Royal Blue or Midnight Blue brocade cloth. Paul will not be able to obtain the Wedgewood Blue brocade cloth until the Tuesday after Easter.

This contract will fail because the parties cannot agree on the color of the seat covers nor can they reach a meeting of the minds or mutual assent s to the delivery date of the seat covers. These two items are critical elements because if Carrie cannot have the color that she wants and the delivery date that she requires then there is no meeting of the minds and hence no contract.

Consideration

Consideration is a term that always causes problems for new legal students. All of our lives we have been taught that consideration refers to the act of being kind and thoughtful towards others. Whereas that is a good definition in most circumstances, in the legal world consideration means something entirely different.

The legal definition of consideration refers to money or something of value that is exchanged or bargained for in contracts and agreements. If a contract does not have the element of consideration it usually fails as a contract at that point it becomes a gift between two or more individuals not a contract. For example, if someone offers me his $12,000 bicycle in exchange for my antique samurai sword, then we probably have a contract. However, if Annie gives her granddaughter a new Mercedes sports car because she turned 16, then consideration is missing and the contract will fail for lack of consideration.

The Parol Evidence Rule

The Parol Evidence Rule simply prevents a party from introducing oral evidence that would change, modify or nullify the terms of a written contract. In some cases, parties try to change or expand the terms of the written contract by stating that the other party promised something else that was not included in the written contract. For example, Daisy and Dudley entered into a written contract whereby they agreed that Dudley would sell Daisy all of the female piglets of his sow's first litter. As luck would have it, none of the female piglets of the first litter survived. Daisy tries to introduce oral evidence that Dudley told her that he would sell her all of the piglets of the first litter. Her statements would be barred by the Parol evidence rule.

Breach of Contract

Breach of contract simply means that one or more parties failed to fulfill their end of the bargain, or broke their promise to the other party. For example, Tooty entered into a contract with Wanda whereby Wanda would type Tooty's research papers for 25 dollars each. If Wanda typed Tooty's two last minute papers but Tooty refused to pay her, then Wanda would allege that Tooty had broken her promise or breached their contract.

Contract Remedies

There are a number of contract remedies; some involve monetary compensation, others involve injunctions and still others involve requiring a party to perform a specific action. The remedies are generally referred to as either money damages or equitable damages.

Monetary Damages

Money damages are fairly straightforward. A party has breached contract and the other party or parties want monetary compensation for the breach. Compensatory damages, which include general and special damages, are the monetary damages usually awarded. Punitive damages are rarely awarded in breach of contract cases.

Compensatory Damages

Compensatory damages or actual damages represented the loss that the non-breaching party suffered as a result of the breach of contract. The compensatory damages are designed to help make the party whole again. General damages directly cover the loss that was suffered and special damages also called (consequential damages) are awarded if the non-breaching party can show that the breaching party knew that the breach of contract would cause more harm than normally would be foreseeable. The losses covered under special damages are generally not the direct or immediate result of the breach of contract.

The Equitable Remedies

Contract rescission, contract reformation and specific performance are known as "equitable remedies."

Contract rescission

Contract rescission allows a former contract to be cancelled or destroyed, then allows for another contract that is more in keeping with the parties' requirements to be created.

Contract reformation

Contract reformation is often used when there has been a term of the contract that was mistaken by both parties. The contract is then redrawn or reformed because there was a mutual mistake that was not intentionally created or manipulated by either party.

Specific performance

Specific performance is a very unusual remedy that is not used as frequently as in past years. Specific performance is a remedy that requires a party to fulfill his or her part of the bargain. Specific performance was used for real property and unique items in the past. For example, if Jimmy promised to sell 5 acres of his farm land to Sam, the court could order Jimmy to sell Sam that 5 acres because land is unique and cannot be replaced or exchanged. The court would not have ordered specific performance if Jimmy contracted to sell an iPhone to Sam because an iPhone is not unique and Sam could obtain the same phone from someone else or a store for the same price or less.

Terms to know:

- Detrimental reliance: one party must make a credible promise and the other party must rely, act or refrain from acting based upon the statements made by the first party. The aggrieved party must have suffered some harm from his or her reliance on the statements.
- Quantum meruit: refers to the real or actual value of services performed. This concept usually comes into play when there is a quasi-contract so that one party is not unjustly enriched at the other party's expense.

Judgment and Analytical Ability

This section of the exam tests the paralegal's analytical and critical thinking skills as well as his or her ability to exercise "good" judgment in professional and personal settings. This section has an essay question that tests the paralegal's reading and comprehension skills as well as his or her analytical skills. A paralegal's ability to write clear, concise prose will determine how well he or she does on the essay question.

One of the best ways to prepare for the essay question is not only to read the questions provided in the study manual, but to read articles, essays and editorials in the regular course of business. Once you have read the materials, write down a synopsis of the main concepts that were discussed in the article. This study tactic works better with at least one other person because the other person can provide feedback as to points and issues the paralegal may have overlooked or misunderstood. The reading and the writing of the synopsis should be timed. There is a twenty-five minute time limit for the judgment and analytical ability section on the test. This section also includes number sequence, logic and analytical reasoning questions that must be answered within that twenty-five minute time frame. Therefore, a paralegal should practice reading and writing the synopsis in less than fifteen minutes.

The more questions that a paralegal completes before the exam, the better his or her chances are of passing. This correlation holds true on the Bar exam as well as other standardized tests. One of the main reasons that practice makes perfect is practice produces speed and accuracy, which are both necessary on timed exams. Constant, repetitive practice trains the eyes and the mind to read, focus, comprehend and process the material much faster than he or she normally would. This is crucial because many people fail exams not because they don't know the material, but because they run out of time. Training one's mind by completing a large amount of practice questions will increase the test takers speed and more than likely his or her score on this timed test.

Also on this section's exam are questions that test the ability to exercise judgment. The questions in this section can be very similar to the Ethics section questions in that if a paralegal follows the rules of ethical conduct on her job, she more than likely will be able to exercise "good" judgment in most instances. It would be effective to study the Canons of Professional Responsibility in order to prepare for this section's questions also.

A good elementary math book or math website will help prepare the paralegal for the number sequence problems that are on the test. If you are not brushed up in this area, it might be a good idea to find a good website or math book and complete at least 50 of the number sequence problems per week in the time leading up to the exam.

If the paralegal follows the suggestions given, completes the practice tests and maintains a thorough study schedule, then he or she will more than likely pass this exam with a minimum of stress.

Practice Exam

1. Definition of Slang:
    a. a type of language that consists of words and phrases that are regarded as very informal, are more common in speech than writing, and are typically restricted to a particular context or group of people.
    b. a word or phrase that is not formal or literary, typically one used in ordinary or familiar conversation
    c. a mild or indirect word or expression substituted for one considered to be too harsh or blunt when referring to something unpleasant or embarrassing.
    d. special words or expressions that are used by a particular profession or group and are difficult for others to understand.

2. Definition of Jargon:
    a. a type of language that consists of words and phrases that are regarded as very informal, are more common in speech than writing, and are typically restricted to a particular context or group of people.
    b. a word or phrase that is not formal or literary, typically one used in ordinary or familiar conversation
    c. a mild or indirect word or expression substituted for one considered to be too harsh or blunt when referring to something unpleasant or embarrassing
    d. special words or expressions that are used by a particular profession or group and are difficult for others to understand.

3. Definition of Colloquialism:
    a. a type of language that consists of words and phrases that are regarded as very informal, are more common in speech than writing, and are typically restricted to a particular context or group of people.
    b. a word or phrase that is not formal or literary, typically one used in ordinary or familiar conversation
    c. a local or regional saying
    d. special words or expressions that are used by a particular profession or group and are difficult for others to understand.

4. The phrase "He is as broke as Job's Turkey" is considered...
    a. foreign speech
    b. a euphemism
    c. a colloquialism
    d. jargon

5. ______ is a verb that means to bring about a chance or to exert influence over a matter.
    a. affect
    b. affectation
    c. running
    d. slacks

6. _______ is a noun that describes the results of an action. Can also be used as a verb that means to cause an action.
    a. affect
    b. effect
    c. positive
    d. smash

7. ______ is a word is a verb that means to receive.
   a. accept
   b. except
   c. run
   d. hit

8. ________ is a preposition that can only be used when referring to two persons, ideas, events etc.
   a. among
   b. between
   c. during
   d. run

9. _______ is a term also can be a noun or a verb that means to give accolades or praise (verb) or it can refer to the actual words of praise (noun).
   a. concise
   b. congest
   c. complement
   d. compliment

10. _______ is a term can be a noun or a verb that means to complete or bring to fruition.
   a. compliment
   b. complement
   c. congruent
   d. conceal

11. _______ is an adjective or adverb that refers to items that cannot be counted separately: air, noise, pollution.
   a. less
   b. many
   c. fewer
   d. about

12. ______ is an adjective used to refer to items that are counted separately
   a. tall
   b. less
   c. fewer
   d. ton

13. _______ is a noun that refers the awareness of right and wrong, good and evil, just and unjust.
   a. come
   b. conscience
   c. conscious
   d. psyche

14. _________ is a descriptive phrase that refers to everyone or everything that is in the last stage of preparation.
   a. alright
   b. already
   c. all ready
   d. beginning

15. ________ is a verb that means cry, sob or weep loudly.
    a. boll
    b. bawl
    c. brawl
    d. laugh

16. __________ names a person, place, thing or idea/concept.
    a. pronoun
    b. verb
    c. adverb
    d. noun

17. A(n)________shows action or state of being.
    a. adverb
    b. adjective
    c. verb
    d. pronoun

18. ________ are defined as words that are used to help the main verb, which is usually an action verb.
    a. articles
    b. adverbs
    c. adjectives
    d. auxiliary verbs

19. ____________ mood is just the basic verb form without regard to tense, number, or any other conjugations to link this form to the subject. Example: to be
    a. infinitive
    b. indicative
    c. subjective
    d. relative

20. ___________ mood is used to convey a command, and the word "you" is most often implied instead of written. Example: Keep Still.
    a. indicative
    b. subjective
    c. imperative
    d. relative

21. _________ conveys the action that the subject is performing.
    a. passive voice
    b. imperative mood
    c. active voice
    d. relative

22. __________ indicates that someone or something else is acting on the subject.
    a. subjective voice
    b. active voice
    c. indicative mood
    d. passive voice

23. "I attached the letter to the email" is an example of the _________.
    a. passive Voice
    b. active Voice
    c. no voice
    d. euphemism

24. "The letter was attached to the email" is an example of the__________.
    a. active Voice
    b. subjective Voice
    c. slang voice
    d. passive Voice

25. The office was a nightmare for the paralegal______ law books were all over the floor, case files were strewn across the desk, and the chair was stacked with unopened mail.
    a. :
    b. ;
    c. ,
    d. .

26. The lady who won the beauty contest had all of the following_____ beautiful face, gorgeous hair, a fit body, and an extensive vocabulary.
    a. ;
    b. ,
    c. .
    d. :

27. Two hundred students applied for law school_____ only fifty of the students were accepted.
    a. ;
    b. ,
    c. :
    d. ()

28. Chuck spoke with this wife, who could not understand him _____ his best friend, who envied him______ his children who disliked him_____ and his attorney, who did not trust him_____ before he declined the offer.
    a. []
    b. ,
    c. ;
    d. :

29. Her large____ Antebellum____ house looked like Tara from "Gone With the Wind".
    a. ;
    b. :
    c. [ ]
    d. !

30. ___________ are also used to link two main clauses if the second clause is an explanation.
    a. semicolons
    b. colons
    c. periods
    d. question marks

31. ___________ should be used to link two main clauses, provided they are not joined by a coordinating conjunction.
   a. commas
   b. apostrophe
   c. semicolons
   d. periods

32. __________ can be used to denote emphasis.
   a. semicolons
   b. colons
   c. commas
   d. exclamation marks

33. ____________ is used to form contractions.
   a. apostrophe
   b. comma
   c. semicolon
   d. period

34. ____________ is to show possession for all singular and indefinite pronouns.
   a. colon
   b. semi-colon
   c. apostrophe
   d. comma

35. Ab- means
   a. away, from
   b. all over, all around
   c. negation, removal, expulsion
   d. outside, beyond

36. infra- means
   a. during
   b. above
   c. below
   d. across

37. pre-
   a. across
   b. before in time, place, order or importance
   c. below
   d. after

38. ex-
   a. out, upward, completely, previous
   b. below
   c. because
   d. bring into the condition of

39. contra-
    a. against, opposite
    b. opposition, opposite direction
    c. having, covered with
    d. in the process of, in a particular state

40. ante-
    a. Because
    b. opposite
    c. before, preceding
    d. in the process of

41. cede-, ceed-, cess-
    a. give up, yield
    b. halt
    c. during
    d. fast

42. dis-
    a. through, between, apart, across
    b. apart, away, not, to the opposite
    c. circle, ring
    d. lead

43. extra, extro-
    a. bear, bring, carry
    b. in front of, previous, earlier
    c. outside, beyond
    d. good, well

44. fore-
    a. in front of, previous, earlier
    b. shape
    c. flower
    d. break

45. effulgence means:
    a. ugly
    b. greedy
    c. bright
    d. passion

46. denouement means:
    a. the end
    b. the part of the story in which the plot is resolved
    c. announcement
    d. proper

47. fugacious means
    a. porcine
    b. bovine
    c. canine
    d. none of the above

48. nugatory means:
    a. having no power or importance
    b. nutty flavor
    c. brain matter
    d. car part

49. puerile means:
    a. bad odor
    b. childish
    c. evil
    d. none of the above

50. virago means:
    a. cat nip
    b. skin disease
    c. washed out areas
    d. a heroine

51. To paraphrase what a witness has stated will:
    a. let him or her know you were listening
    b. make him or her angry
    c. will cause confusion between facts and events
    d. get you in trouble with your boss

52. Although the paralegal is not an attorney, before, during and after the interview the paralegal must stress that the interview is:
    a. a time to have fun
    b. confidential
    c. both a and b
    d. none of the above

53. A hostile witness is
    a. a former criminal
    b. pugilistic
    c. one that may give testimony detrimental to your case
    d. all of the above

Judgment and Analytical Ability

Read the following, then answer the questions.

Margaret is a paralegal who has over twenty-five years of experience, which includes ten years of experience as legal secretary. She recently accepted a position at a firm that specializes in discovery work. There is a lot of new technology that she has never worked with, but she has always prided herself on her ability to learn new concepts quickly. Margaret has been quickly picking up the new information and everyone is pleased by her progress.

Due to the nature of the work, there are days in which she can accomplish very little until the tech support folks iron out the problems. There are also days in which overtime is offered because deadlines must be met. Chris, Margaret's immediate supervisor explained the "feast or famine" workload to Margaret during her job interview. Margaret understood this but she believes that Chris and Cindy, who is Chris' boss, are just young and lazy and do not really know how to manage the workflow.

Margaret tells Chris that she would like extra work and Chris informs her that there is nothing that can be done until the error in the system is cleared up. Not satisfied with Chris' answer, Margaret goes to Cindy, Chris's supervisor , who summarily dismisses her and tells her to go back to her office and "cool her jets." Margaret is incensed at the way she was treated by these young women and she is thinking about either telling the managing partner about the incidents or submitting her resignation, even though she loves her new job.

54. In the light of the events that transpired, Margaret should
    a. Resign immediately
    b. Complain to the managing partner
    c. Wait out the time as the other staff does during the "famine" work flow time
    d. File complaints with the Bar association against Chris and Cindy

55. Based on the facts presented above, Margaret has grounds to bring a suit for
    a. sex discrimination
    b. age discrimination
    c. sexual Harrassment
    d. none of the above

56. Beaujolais is to wine as
    a. gumbo is to crackers
    b. Arizona Iced Tea is to soft drink
    c. fat is to robust
    d. mug is to beer

57. Annie and Kerry have been friends for years. Annie used to have a drinking and substance abuse problem but had been "clean" for about six years. Lately, Kerry has noticed that significant amounts of the petty cash money has been disappearing. She also has noticed that Annie has been eating her lunch alone in her office everyday instead of joining other paralegals on their restaurant tours. Kerry suspects that Annie may have restarted her bad habits. Kerry should:
    a. talk to Annie's boss about the problem
    b. call Annie's husband and tell him her suspicions
    c. confront Annie and tell her that if she doesn't come clean Kerry will report the missing money
    d. do nothing since she does not have proof that Annie has done anything wrong.

58. A paralegal is to an attorney as a
    a. nurse is to a doctor
    b. agent is to an actor
    c. A physician's assistant is to a doctor
    d. a legal secretary is to an attorney

59. Jackie has an interview at Dawson and Dooney, the swankiest law firm in town. Everyone at the firm dresses well and drives luxury cars. Jackie has been unemployed for a while, so her funds are really low. Her interview suit is too small and nearly threadbare and her car is a rust heap. Jackie knows she only has one chance to make a good impression and she wants to spend her last 200 dollars well. She should:
    a. skip the interview and look for a job at a lower profile firm
    b. max out her last credit card to rent a luxury car for the interview and buy a new suit that will make a lasting impression.
    c. buy a new interview suit but take a taxi to the interview, which will save her 100 dollars
    d. put on her old suit and jogging shoes and walk to the interview; she can explain that she believes daily exercise is essential for productive work.

60. 7. What is the next number in this series? 3, 6, 12, 24, 4, 8, 16, 32 ...?
    a. 2
    b. 7
    c. 10
    d. 5

61. How many years will it take Lucy to have over 20,000 dollars in the bank if she currently has 12,000 dollars and the interest rate is 3%?
    a. 2 years
    b. 17 years
    c. 30 years
    d. 18 years

62. slope is equal to
    a. height times width
    b. rise over run
    c. the sum of the angles
    d. all of the above

Ethics

63. If a client asks a paralegal for legal advice, what should the paralegal do?
    a. Advise the client
    b. Tell the client about another attorney's office
    c. Tell him to speak to her boss because she is prohibited from advising clients
    d. Do nothing

64. If a client wants to pay the paralegal as a bonus for all the help that she has given him, what should the paralegal do?
    a. Take the money and tell the attorney
    b. Take the money and keep it a secret
    c. Do nothing
    d. Tell the client she is prohibited from taking personal fees.

65. If a paralegal is made aware of a confidential lucrative deal to help a family member, he should do what?
    a. do nothing
    b. ask the boss what to do
    c. tell the family member secretly
    d. introduce the family member to the client

66. Which one of these duties is not ethical for a paralegal to perform?
    a. Shepardize
    b. conduct Legal Research
    c. advise the client
    d. perform administrative duties

67. Which kind of client can a paralegal work with?
    a. her cousin
    b. her former boss
    c. a total stranger
    d. her Mother

68. If a client breaks a non-violent law, what should the paralegal do?
    a. call the police
    b. report the incident to her boss (the attorney assigned to the case)
    c. do nothing
    d. tell opposing counsel

69. A Chinese Wall is...
    a. a big stone wall that keeps out invading Mongols
    b. necessary to isolate legal staff that may have a conflict due to prior exposure
    c. a derogatory racist slur
    d. none of the above

70. An attorney and a paralegal can split the legal fees...
    a. never
    b. if the client agrees
    c. as long as the attorney get the larger amount
    d. b and c

71. Commingling funds means...
    a. playing the stock market
    b. keeping client funds that have not been authorized for spending with personal funds
    c. keeping foreign and US money in the same bank
    d. putting rental income in same account as work income

72. Barry, who is married, has been having a secret affair with the new paralegal at the firm around the corner. He has no intent to leave his wife but if his affair is revealed, he can be found guilty of which violation?
    a. moral turpitude
    b. conflict of interest
    c. burglary
    d. embezzlement

73. Gina finally met the man of her dreams and they have been dating for the last two weeks while they were on a cruise. When Gina walked into a case management meeting on Monday, she was shocked to discover that her dream man is a senior paralegal at the firm with which she has a big case coming up. She is now worried whether she may have said something about the case to him. He wants to continue dating. Gina should...
    a. find a new job and marry him
    b. do nothing
    c. advise her managing attorney of the possible conflict
    d. Accuse him of buttering her up just to get info on the case.

74. Patty has taken the bar eight times in three different states and has failed. She is ashamed and miserable, but all of her friends and family think that she is a licensed attorney. Her cousin Sheila comes to her for assistance, Patty is too embarrassed to tell Sheila that she never passed the bar, so although she does not accept money from Sheila, she completes the work that Sheila needs done in the same manner that an attorney would. Patty is guilty of...
    a. Unauthorized practice of law
    b. nothing because Sheila is family and she is allowed to help family members
    c. nothing because she did not accept a fee
    d. both b and c

75. Rhonda loves emeralds and has several that she purchased for herself. A client sends Rhonda a large emerald worth about 25,000 dollars. What should she do about the emerald?
    a. keep it and wear it proudly
    b. give it back
    c. secretly keep it and not let anyone know who gave it to her.
    d. pawn it and go on a vacation.

76. Ginger's uncle Will is the chief judge in Clickle, MA. She is his favorite niece and he is her favorite uncle. Every Friday they go to happy hour and then to dinner. Ginger just became the new assistant district attorney for the area in which Uncle hears cases. How does this affect Uncle Will and Ginger?
    a. It does not. After all, they are family and have been having dinner and drinks together for years
    b. Uncle Will should recuse himself on cases in which Ginger is the attorney to avoid the appearance of impropriety.
    c. Ginger should find another job in a different city.
    d. Ginger should use her relationship with Uncle Will to gain advantage over opposing counsel.

77. In order for a licensed attorney to practice law in another state, he or she must either become a member of the state's bar or
    a. file to proceed in forma pauperis
    b. do nothing because he or she is already licensed in one state
    c. go to law school in that new state and get another degree
    d. file to proceed *pro hac vice*

Legal Research

78. Corpus Delicti means:
    a. the body of the crime
    b. delightful dessert
    c. dead body
    d. none of the above

79. Ex Post Facto means:
   a. before the fact
   b. near the post office
   c. contrary to the facts
   d. after the fact

80. Furtum means:
   a. theft or something stolen
   b. a fugitive
   c. an insect
   d. Allen wrench

81. Ipso facto means:
   a. like a spider
   b. drunk or tipsy
   c. by the act itself
   d. watchword

82. Quid Pro Quo means:
   a. something for nothing
   b. this for that
   c. a small baby squid
   d. a yoga position

83. ____________ is defined as the authority or power that a court has to hear a specific type of case.
   a. venue
   b. jurisdiction
   c. voir dire
   d. laissez-faire

84. _________ is a Latin term that refers to an order sent by the court requiring a witness to appear and bring specified evidence.
   a. hostile witness
   b. subpoena duces tecum
   c. sua sponte
   d. in limine

85. _________ is a sworn statement that is notarized.
   a. counterclaim
   b. citation
   c. affidavit
   d. ex parte

86. _______ this term used to indicate the challenge to the plaintiff's allegations.
   a. demurrer
   b. hearsay Evidence
   c. ex parte
   d. long arm statute

87. __________ refers to a decision made by the court when a defendant does not answer the plaintiff's complaint within the allotted timeframe.

a. demurrer
b. long arm statute
c. hearsay Evidence
d. default judgment

88. Statements made by anyone outside of court and not under oath are an example of ______________.

a. hostile witness
b. ex parte
c. hearsay evidence
d. in limine

89. _________ is a motion for a new trial when the judge fails to correct and error or makes an error.

a. sua sponte
b. motion for trial de novo
c. demurrer
d. voir dire

90. ___________ refers to the grounds for dismissal of a cause of action because the location in which the matter was filed would be inconvenient for the defendant.

a. long arm statute
b. hostile witness
c. forum non convenience
d. replevin

91. A common law remedy that requires that property that was illegally or wrongly taken from a party be returned to the rightful owner is called a(n) ____________.

a. sua sponte
b. subpoena duces tecum
c. replevin
d. in limine

92. Laws that allow causes of actions to be brought against nonresidents in some instances are called_________.

a. short arm statute
b. ex parte
c. long arm statute
d. extradition

93. ________ is a Latin term that refers to decisions made by the judge without motion or requests from either party. In essence these types of decisions are made by the judge voluntarily based on his own discretion.

a. motion for trial de novo
b. in Limine
c. sua sponte
d. voir dire

94. ________ is the term given for a cause of action brought by a defendant and is submitted with the defendant's answer to the plaintiff's complaint.
   a. motion for trial de novo
   b. sua Sponte
   c. counterclaim
   d. default judgment

95. It is best to use a tertiary source when _______.
   a. the case number is already known.
   b. a paralegal is given a term that he or she does not know and is asked to find out the latest information on the topic.
   c. the paralegal is provided the citation or identifying page numbers of original cases that have provided decisions.
   d. the paralegal feels like it.

96. It is best to use a secondary source when _______.
   a. the case number is already known.
   b. a paralegal is given a term that he or she does not know and is asked to find out the latest information on the topic.
   c. the paralegal is provided the citation or identifying page numbers of original cases that have provided decisions.
   d. the paralegal feels like it.

97. It is best to use a primary source when _______.
   a. the case number is already known.
   b. a paralegal is given a term that he or she does not know and is asked to find out the latest information on the topic.
   c. the paralegal is provided the citation or identifying page numbers of original cases that have provided decisions.
   d. the paralegal feels like it.

98. __________ refers to the huge, master index to all US case law. This set of reference materials is published by Thomson/West. It is comprised of the Century Digest, the General Digest and the Decennial Digests.
   a. Corpus Juris Secondum
   b. Code of Federal Regulations
   c. American Digest System
   d. American Law Reports

99. ___________ is a secondary source (group of annotations) that explains the differences in application of legal topics and laws in various jurisdictions.
   a. Atlantic Reporter
   b. American Law Reports
   c. Corpus Juris Secondum
   d. Legal Research

100. ____________ is a legal research source called a citatory that provides a complete and comprehensive list of all cases that have mentioned or cited a particular case.
   a. American Law Reports
   b. Shepard's Citations
   c. Decennial Digest
   d. Corpus Juris Secondum

101. ____________is a legal encyclopedia published by West Publishing that uses the West Key system, allowing for cross-indexing and searching from encyclopedia to digests to reporters.
   a. Legal Research
   b. American Law Reports
   c. American Jurisprudence
   d. Primary Source

102. ____________ is a consolidation and codification by subject matter of the general and permanent laws of the United States. It is prepared by the Office of the Law Revision Counsel of the United States House of Representatives
   a. Code of Federal Regulations
   b. United States Code
   c. United States Constitution
   d. Legal Research

103. The Constitution, Statutes, Administrative Regulations and decisions from the highest courts in a specified jurisdiction, i.e., US Supreme Court, Kansas Supreme Court or the New Hampshire Court of Appeals are examples of____________.
   a. primary source
   b. secondary source
   c. fourth source
   d. open source

104. Digests, Citators and Restatements plus other legal books and databases are examples of ____________.
   a. primary authority
   b. secondary authority
   c. no authority
   d. fourth authority

Substantive Law

105. The following are types of cases usually heard in Federal court except____________________.
   a. bankruptcy cases
   b. cases involving ambassadors and ministers
   c. cases involving the constitutionality of a law
   d. traffic violations

106. Federal courts obtain their funding from__________________.
   a. Federal government to keep their objectivity
   b. A slush fund from the states
   c. State governments
   d. The President funds the federal court system.

107. _______________ means the plaintiff must be the one who was actually harmed.

a. sitting
b. jurisdiction
c. standing
d. hearsay

108. If your friend is cheated out of his money by a car salesman, __________ can sue the car salesman.

a. you
b. his parents
c. you and your friend
d. only your friend

109. I need to declare bankruptcy. Therefore, I should go to ________________.

a. any Federal court
b. Family Law court
c. Bankruptcy court
d. Bankruptcy and criminal court

110. A federal case must (be/have) ______________ or have an active or ongoing legal issue that needs to be addressed in order for the Federal Courts to hear the case.

a. old
b. moot
c. standing
d. in the future

111. Federal question jurisdiction refers to_______________.

a. Cases that involve disputes between two parties
b. Cases that involve disputes between two or more states, cases that involve disputes between the United States and foreign governments, or cases that present questions in relation to the US Constitution, the US Government or Federal laws
c. Class action cases
d. Corporate Law cases

112. A case involving a remedy to be paid no later than a past date will be thrown out because ...?

a. it is declared to have mootness
b. it lacks standing
c. it violates the balance of the harms
d. no reason

113. West Virginia is suing Ohio, claiming Ohio dumped toxic pollution in the waters of West Virginia. Which court would it go to?

a. State Court
b. Municipal Court
c. Federal Court
d. Bankruptcy Court

114. There are _____ circuit courts in the DC Circuit in the US court of Appeals System

a. 13
b. 6
c. 11
d. 15

115. Puerto Rico, though not a state, is in the _____ circuit.
   a. DC circuit
   b. 8th circuit
   c. 4th circuit
   d. 1st circuit

116. The executive branch_________________.
   a. Is comprised of the US Supreme Court, the Federal courts and the state courts.
   b. Consists of the US Congress and the state legislative bodies of each state. The Senate and the House of Representatives make up the Congress.
   c. Is made up of the President of the United States, each state's governor and the Administrative agencies' chief executives.
   d. Is the most powerful branch in government and controls spending.

117. A paralegal would be most likely to work in the _____________ branch of government.
   a. Executive
   b. Legislative
   c. Judicial
   d. Parliamentary

118. Marbury v. Madison decided____________________
   a. the right to use birth control
   b. the doctrine of judicial review
   c. abolished miscegenation and interracial marriage prohibition laws
   d. gave women the right to obtain legal abortion

119. Loving v. Virginia, decided in 1967, ____________________
   a. established the right to use birth control
   b. abolished miscegenation and interracial marriage prohibition laws
   c. denounced segregation in schools
   d. Established women's right to vote

120. The Supreme Court grants a _______________ to hear a case.
   a. discovery
   b. writ of Admission
   c. writ of Certiorari
   d. demurrer

121. ________ is the highest court in the nation:
   a. appellate Court
   b. municipal Court
   c. Congress
   d. the United States Supreme Court

122. __________ was the first female Justice:
   a. Elena Kagan
   b. Sandra Day O'Connor
   c. Sonia Sotomayor
   d. Hilary Clinton

123. The first African American Justice to serve on the Supreme Court was________________.

   a. Clarence Thomas
   b. Thurmond Marshall.
   c. Samuel Alito
   d. Jackson Miller

124. The Bill of Rights is comprised of the first____ amendments to the Constitution

   a. 2
   b. 5
   c. 16
   d. 10

125. The Constitutional Convention met in Philadelphia for _________ in order to create the Constitution.

   a. 12 days
   b. 12 years
   c. 3 ½ months
   d. none of the above

126. The legislative branch__________________.

   a. Consists of the US Congress and the state legislative bodies of each state.
   b. Is comprised of the US Supreme Court, the Federal courts and the state courts.
   c. Is made up of the President of the United States and the governors
   d. Is the parliamentary system for the US.

127. The judicial branch__________________.

   a. Consists of the US Congress and the state legislative bodies of each state.
   b. Is made up of the President of the United States, the Administrative agencies' chiefs.
   c. Is comprised of the US Supreme Court, the Federal courts and the state courts.
   d. Is the Super Presidential system.

128. The Due Process Clause Protects the following, except:_____________.

   a. compensation for takings
   b. double Jeopardy
   c. not being compelled to witness against one's self.
   d. right to bear arms

129. The police jail a man without a trial for 20 years. This is an example of a violation of the

_________________.

   a. Commerce Clause
   b. Due Process Clause
   c. Establishment Clause
   d. There is no violation

130. The Establishment Clause is defined as__________________.

   a. The federal government has the right to regulate commerce.
   b. No citizen shall have their life liberty or property taken without due process.
   c. Congress shall make no law respecting an establishment of religion, or prohibiting the free exercise thereof; or abridging the freedom of speech, or of the press; or the right of the people peaceably to assemble, and to petition the Government for a redress of grievance.
   d. The Federal government has total sovereignty over its Citizens.

131. Double Jeopardy is defined as_______________.
   a. The freedom to bear arms
   b. The freedom from being tried twice for the same crime
   c. The freedom to remain silent
   d. The freedom of the press

132. The Freedom to assemble is protected by the ______________.
   a. Commerce Clause
   b. Due Process Clause
   c. Free Exercise Clause
   d. Establishment Clause

133. How does the 14th amendment relate to the Due Process Clause?
   a. gives the Federal Government the right to regulate trade
   b. gives the government the right to take away all property
   c. gives citizens the right to a speedy trial
   d. says that states must adhere to Due Process.

134. What is Due Process?
   a. The right to free press
   b. Administrative law
   c. A fair trial or proceeding
   d. The right to assemble

135. Freedom of speech is protected by the ______________.
   a. Establishment Clause
   b. Due Process Clause
   c. Commerce Clause
   d. Contract Clause

136. If the Federal Government passed a law discriminating against Christians, this would be violate the _________of the Constitution.
   a. Establishment Clause
   b. Due Process Clause
   c. Commerce Clause
   d. Freedom Clause

137. ____________ protects your right as an American citizen to petition your government.
   a. The First Amendment under the Establishment Clause
   b. The Second Amendment under the Establishment Clause
   c. The Twenty-eighth Amendment under the Establishment Clause
   d. The Tenth Amendment under the Establishment Clause

138. Procedural Due Process is defined as____________.
   a. a course of formal proceedings (as legal proceedings) carried out regularly and in accordance with established rules and principles
   b. a judicial requirement that enacted laws may not contain provisions that result in the unfair, arbitrary, or unreasonable treatment of an individual.
   c. The right to petition your government
   d. The right to be free from illegal searches and seizers.

139. Substantive due process is________________________.
    a. a course of formal proceedings (legal proceedings) carried out regularly and in accordance with established rules and principles
    b. the right to the Establishment Clause
    c. The right to vote.
    d. a judicial requirement that enacted laws may not contain provisions that result in the unfair, arbitrary, or unreasonable treatment of an individual.

140. A US born terrorist's access to his rights as a citizen is considered __________________.
    a. Procedural Law issue
    b. Substantive Law issue
    c. Military law issue
    d. State and local law issue

141. An example of a state's seizure of a suspected drug dealer's car involves what type of Due Process?
    a. Procedural
    b. Factual
    c. Substantive
    d. Health

142. Due Process was first written in the_____________.
    a. Pentagon Papers
    b. British Magna Carta
    c. Declaration of Independence
    d. United States Constitution

Business Organizations

143. A sole proprietorship is defined as ______________.
    a. Two or more owners of a business who agree to be liable for the debts of the partnership/business
    b. An unincorporated business owned and run by one individual (no partners are involved), with no distinction between the business and its owner.
    c. Hybrid type of legal structure that provides the limited liability features of a corporation and the tax efficiencies and operational flexibility of a partnership whose "owners" are referred to as "members".
    d. An illegal business

144. Who or what is legally and financially responsible for a sole proprietorship?
    a. The Board
    b. The owner of the business
    c. Shareholders
    d. Government

145. One disadvantage to having a sole proprietorship is_____________.
    a. Flexible work hours
    b. The owner keeps all the profits
    c. The owner is personally liable for the actions of the business
    d. The owner does not have a lot of paper work

146. One great advantage to a sole proprietorship is_____________.
   a. The owner is liable for everything
   b. It is difficult to obtain a loan
   c. The owner keeps all the profits
   d. You must be good at accounting

147. A general partnership consists of_________________.
   a. a board where the government is held responsible
   b. partners that are only liable to the extent of their contribution to the partnership
   c. a board that is responsible for all actions
   d. two or more owners of a business who agree to be liable for the debts of the partnership/business

148. A limited partnership consists of _____________________.
   a. a board that is responsible for all actions
   b. partners are only liable to the extent of their contribution to the partnership
   c. a board where the government is held responsible
   d. two or more owners of a business who agree to be liable for the debts of the partnership/business

149. If you go into business with risky partners, which partnership is best?
   a. A general partnership
   b. Government partnership
   c. Limited Partnership
   d. Triple partnership

150. If you go into business with financially conservative partner, which partnership is best?
   a. Government Partnership
   b. Limited Partnership
   c. General Partnership
   d. Triple Partnership

151. In a Limited Partnership, partners give up_____________.
   a. Control of daily operations
   b. All income
   c. All direction of the business
   d. nothing

152. A Limited Liability Company is defined as _____________________.
   a. A "hybrid type of legal structure that provides the limited liability features of a corporation and the tax efficiencies and operational flexibility of a partnership whose "owners" are referred to as "members."
   b. an unincorporated business owned and run by one individual (no partners are involved), with no distinction between the business and its owner.
   c. two or more owners of a business who agree to be liable for the debts of the partnership/business
   d. An illegal venture

153. ___________usually includes percentage of interests, allocation of profits and losses, member's rights and responsibilities and other provisions for a LLC.
   a. Articles of Organization
   b. Operating agreement
   c. Joint venture
   d. Constitution

154. ___________ is a business arrangement in which two or more parties agree to pool their resources for the purpose of accomplishing a specific task. This task can be a new project or any other business activity.

a. corporation
b. LLC
c. joint venture
d. government

155. A joint venture ________.

a. Can be terminated when someone dies or there is no economic interest
b. Can never be terminated
c. Can never be terminated because it is considered a living person
d. Can only be terminated by the government

156. ____________permitted venturers involved in joint research and development to notify the government of their joint venture and thus limit their liability in the event of prosecution for antitrust violations.

a. National Cooperative Research Act of 1984
b. Export Trading Company Act
c. Sherman Anti-Trust Act
d. United States Constitution

157. Securities are______________________.

a. rules set by corporations
b. government issued regulations
c. shares of stock, bonds, and debentures issued by corporations and governments
d. permits to open a corporation

158. ________________are debt instruments that can be bought or sold between two parties and have basic terms defined, such as notional amount (amount borrowed), interest rate and maturity/renewal date.

a. Securities
b. Stocks
c. Debt securities
d. Dividends

159. ___________________include any stock or similar security, certificate of interest or participation in any profit sharing agreement, preorganization certificate or subscription, transferable share, voting trust certificate or certificate of deposit for an equity security, limited partnership interest, interest in a joint venture, or certificate of interest in a business trust; any security future on any such security; or any security convertible, with or without consideration into such a security, or carrying any warrant or right to subscribe to or purchase such a security; or any such warrant or right; or any put, call, straddle, or other option or privilege of buying such a security from or selling such a security to another without being bound to do so.

a. Securities
b. Equity securities
c. CDs
d. CDOs

160. Securities are regulated by the___________________.

a. Securities and Exchange Commission
b. Department of Transportation
c. Secretary of State
d. President of the United States

161. Stocks, certificates of interest, dividend-bearing stocks or profit sharing agreements are called____________.
   a. Debt Securities
   b. Collateralized debt obligations
   c. Equity Securities
   d. Bonds

162. ____________include government bonds, corporate bonds, CDs, municipal bonds, preferred stock, collateralized securities.
   a. Debt Securities
   b. Collateralized debt obligations
   c. Equity Securities
   d. Stocks

163. The owners of equity securities are called____________.
   a. Shareholders
   b. Chief Executive Officers
   c. Bond holders
   d. Vice President of Finance

164. ______________ is often referred to as the "truth in securities" law. It has two basic objectives. 1. Require that investors receive financial and other significant information concerning securities being offered for public sale; and 2. prohibit deceit, misrepresentations, and other fraud in the sale of securities.
   a. Securities Exchange Act of 1934
   b. The Securities Act of 1933
   c. Trust Indenture Act of 1939
   d. Investment Company Act of 1940

165. _________________ regulates the organization of companies, including mutual funds, that engage primarily in investing, reinvesting, and trading in securities, and whose own securities are offered to the investing public.
   a. Investment Company Act of 1940
   b. Investment Advisers Act of 1940
   c. United States Constitution
   d. Sarbanes-Oxley Act of 2002

166. _______________ set out to reshape the U.S. regulatory system in a number of areas including but not limited to consumer protection, trading restrictions, credit ratings, regulation of financial products, corporate governance and disclosure, and transparency.
   a. Jumpstart Our Business Startups Act of 2012
   b. Dodd-Frank Wall Street Reform and Consumer Protection Act of 2010
   c. Securities Exchange Act of 1934
   d. United States Constitution

167. Persons who acquire___________ are granted the usual and traditional rights associated with stock ownership: voting rights, dividends, and claim to the residual assets if there is liquidation.
    a. preferred stock
    b. government bonds
    c. corporate bonds
    d. common stock

168. __________ have cumulative dividends and their dividend is paid first
    a. bonds
    b. common stock
    c. preferred stock
    d. government bonds

169. __________these are stocks from old-line profitable companies. These stocks reflect a sometimes century old record of high and stable earnings. They almost always pay dividends.
    a. common stock
    b. blue chip stock
    c. preferred stock
    d. government bonds

170. __________ are high risk stocks that do not pay a dividend.
    a. growth stocks
    b. penny stocks
    c. blue chip stocks
    d. government bonds

171. _________ can be purchased for as low as a few dollars per share; these stocks are not usually traded on the major exchanges.
    a. penny stocks
    b. growth stocks
    c. dividends
    d. blue chip stocks

172. ___________ are stocks that investors think are being traded lower than their market value and many investors believe that this type of stock can provide long-term growth because the stocks are perceived as undervalued.
    a. blue chip stocks
    b. penny stocks
    c. growth stocks
    d. value stocks

173. ___________ are contracts or agreements that authorize or allow the stockholder to buy or sell shares of stock at a specific price for a specified time frame without having to adhere to the market price for that time.
    a. in the money agreements
    b. stock options
    c. stock splits
    d. out of the money agreements

174. ___________occurs when the number of shares of stock is increased but the value of the shares is decreased.

a. in the money trade
b. stock split
c. stock write off
d. exercising a stock option

175. ___________ is a type of stock with an artificially inflated value above its actual worth.

a. stock option
b. penny stock
c. watered stock
d. fat cat

176. Preemptive rights

a. are given to common stock owners
b. allow the share holder to buy the same proportion of new stock if the company issues new stock as the amount he or she had of the old stock.
c. are given to preferred shareholders
d. both a and b

177. A written proxy...

a. Is illegal
b. keeps outsiders from being able to buy stock
c. allows a shareholder to vote on someone else's behalf
d. promotes embezzlement and ponzi schemes

178. Minority shareholders can vote for one director of their choosing by using or doing the following:

a. cumulative voting
b. voting trusts
c. both a and b
d. none of the above

179. The ______ (is/are) elected at the annual meetings of shareholders

a. corporate officers
b. board of directors
c. shareholders
d. none of the above

180. Piercing the corporate veil means:

a. A legal decision that will strip the corporate owners of their limited liability protection
b. Dissolving the corporation and selling the assets.
c. Moving the corporation to another state
d. Exposing embezzlement by removing “the veil of corruption”

Contracts

181. An executory contract is a...

a. document written for executives
b. contract in which all obligations have been fulfilled
c. contract in which some requirements have not be completed
d. both a and c

182. In contract law, mutual assent takes the form of
  a. offer and acceptance
  b. devise and bequeath
  c. law and order
  d. offer and counteroffer

183. Consideration in a contract means______________.
  a. respect for all of the other parties
  b. location that is agreeable to all
  c. money or something of value
  d. none of the above

184. In a bilateral contract, there is a promise made by
  a. both parties
  b. all parties
  c. no one
  d. one party

185. An express contract...
  a. is usually written
  b. specifically states the terms of the agreement
  c. both a and b
  d. neither a nor b

186. Contracts are considered unenforceable if...
  a. they violate public policy
  b. one or more parties lack the capacity to form a contract
  c. They were made under duress
  d. all of the above

187. The Parol Evidence Rule...
  a. allows a defendant to use new evidence to get paroled early
  b. allows a person to introduce oral evidence that can nullify the written contract
  c. does not allow a party to introduce oral evidence to nullify a written contract
  d. has nothing to do with law

188. If Sharon promises to redecorate Amy's house while Amy and her husband are on honeymoon but instead spends the down payment for the job at the casinos and does not do the work, Amy can...
  a. sue Sharon for breach of contract
  b. cannot get her down payment back
  c. can have Sharon arrested
  d. can punch Sharon in the nose

189. Detrimental reliance means
  a. relying on the government to take of you
  b. a party believed the other party's words and acted or refrained to his/her detriment
  c. filing fraudulent tax returns
  d. none of the above

190. All of these are equitable remedies except
   a. specific performance
   b. contract reformation
   c. contract rescission
   d. wage garnishment

Civil Litigation

191. ____________ is the name given to legal causes of actions that are governed by either the Federal or State Rules of Civil Procedure.
   a. criminal litigation
   b. civil procedure
   c. civil litigation
   d. criminal law

192. ____________ is designed to address torts and other non-violent actions that persons or companies inflict on one another.
   a. Federal court
   b. Civil court
   c. Criminal court
   d. Monkey court

193. ____________ is the term that means more than one court has the authority to hear the specific type of case.
   a. concurrent jurisdiction
   b. venue
   c. jurisdiction
   d. civil Procedure

194. __________ means that a person does not have adequate funds to pay filing fees.
   a. international firing procedure
   b. In Forma Pauperis
   c. SNAP
   d. laissez-faire

195. ___________ is defined as a notice from the court to appear in court and defend the lawsuit. It will be served to the defendant at his or her last known address; therefore, it is very important that the contact information is accurate.
   a. summons
   b. venue
   c. warrant
   d. arrest

196. __________ is comprised of request that documents that are not attorney-client privileged and may be germane to the issues of the case be either copied or made available for inspection for the opposing counsel.
   a. discovery
   b. summons
   c. warrant
   d. voir dire

197. _________ is a means or way for the court to administer justice by awarding a judgment, issuing an injunction or dispensing a penalty.

a. remedy
b. summons
c. warrant
d. arrest

198. Where should a Paralegal look for the court rules?

a. friends in the medical field
b. a website outside the jurisdiction
c. court website for forms
d. a generic form

199. Which of these is *not* a civil court?

a. District small claims court
b. Family court
c. Probate court
d. Federal Criminal Court

200. An interrogatory governed by Rule 33 is

a. a motion for dismissal
b. a judgment in favor of the plaintiff
c. a form of discovery
d. an ad litem guardian

201. A free legal research site is:

a. LEXIS
b. Justia
c. Leagle
d. both b and c

Answer Key

1. A
2. D
3. C
4. C
5. A
6. B
7. A
8. B
9. D
10. B
11. A
12. C
13. B
14. C
15. B
16. D
17. C
18. B
19. A
20. C
21. C
22. D
23. B
24. D
25. A
26. D
27. A
28. B
29. C
30. B
31. C
32. D
33. A
34. C
35. A
36. C
37. B
38. A
39. A
40. C
41. A
42. B
43. C
44. A
45. C
46. B
47. D
48. A
49. B
50. D
51. A
52. B
53. C
54. C
55. D
56. B
57. D
58. A
59. C
60. D
61. D
62. B
63. C
64. D
65. B
66. C
67. C
68. B
69. B
70. A
71. B
72. A
73. C
74. A
75. B
76. B
77. D
78. A
79. D
80. A
81. C
82. B
83. B
84. B

85. C
86. A
87. D
88. C
89. C
90. C
91. C
92. C
93. C
94. C
95. A
96. C
97. B
98. C
99. B
100. B
101. C
102. A
103. A
104. B
105. D
106. A
107. C
108. D
109. C
110. C
111. B
112. A
113. C
114. C
115. D
116. C
117. B
118. B
119. B
120. C
121. D
122. B
123. B
124. D
125. C
126. A
127. C
128. D
129. B
130. C
131. B
132. D
133. D
134. C
135. A
136. A
137. A
138. A
139. D
140. A
141. C
142. B
143. B
144. B
145. C
146. C
147. D
148. B
149. A
150. C
151. D
152. A
153. A
154. C
155. A
156. A
157. C
158. C
159. B
160. A
161. C
162. A
163. A
164. B
165. A
166. B
167. D
168. C
169. B
170. A
171. A
172. D
173. B
174. C
175. C
176. C

177. C
178. A
179. B
180. A
181. C
182. A
183. C
184. A
185. C
186. D
187. C
188. A
189. B
190. B
191. C
192. B
193. A
194. B
195. A
196. A
197. A
198. C
199. D
200. C
201. A